Walter Scott Allerton

A history of the Allerton family in the United States.

1585 to 1885. And a genealogy of the descendants of Isaac Alllerton

Walter Scott Allerton

A history of the Allerton family in the United States.
1585 to 1885. And a genealogy of the descendants of Isaac Aillerton

ISBN/EAN: 9783337723668

Printed in Europe, USA, Canada, Australia, Japan

Cover: Foto ©ninafisch / pixelio.de

More available books at **www.hansebooks.com**

A HISTORY

OF

THE ALLERTON FAMILY

IN THE UNITED STATES.

1585 TO 1885.

AND

A GENEALOGY OF THE DESCENDANTS
OF ISAAC ALLERTON.

BY

WALTER S. ALLERTON.

NEW YORK:
PUBLISHED BY THE AUTHOR.
1888.

P. F. McBreen, Printer,
61 Beekman Street,
New York.

LIST OF PORTRAITS.

Walter S. Allerton (303) . . .	Frontispiece
David Allerton (129) . .	To face page 20
Samuel W. Allerton (60) .	" " 52
Archibald M. Allerton (50) .	" " 68
Mead Allerton (94) .	" " 76
John Russell Allerton (68) .	" " 84
Orville H. Allerton (149) .	" " 100
Samuel W. Allerton (154) . .	" " 108
George W. Allerton (124) . .	" " 116
Orville H. Allerton (348) .	" " 124
Orville H. Allerton (149) . .	" " 132
Ida and Edith Allerton (487, 488)	" " 140

ERRATA.

Page 8, for John[5](13) read John[5] (14).

Page 106, for William Alander, read William Alexander.

Page 143, for Frank V.[9], read Frank H.[9]

Page 144, for Rufus M.[9], read Rufus K.[9]

Page 146, for Amos N.[9], read Amos V.[9]

PREFACE.

PRIDE of ancestry is common to all ages and all peoples, and it is an entirely proper and justifiable sentiment. We know that man, like other animals, possesses the power to transmit to his offspring the mental and physical characteristics that have been most prominent in himself. Students of social science tell us that the children of criminals are apt to prove criminals themselves, and other things being equal, the man who can trace his descent through a dozen generations of honest men is for that very reason more likely to prove himself an honest man.

The history of the Allerton family is a strong proof of the enduring quality of family traits and characteristics, both physical and mental, for we find in members of two branches, that have been entirely separated for two centuries, the same physical appearance and the same mental peculiarities. We find in a majority of the family to-day many resemblances in personal appearance to their common ancestor, and we find still more prominent the same peculiarities of mind and disposition. We are proud to recognize the same spirit of honesty and independence that led him to cast in his lot with the adventurers of New Plymouth, and the same broadness of mind and toleration of the opinions of others that brought him into conflict with the narrow spirit of puritanism. We claim a share of his courage and his enterprise and we admit that we have also inherited somewhat of his quick temper, and of his wandering disposition and unsettled spirit. The Allertons have ever been wanderers, they can point to no one place as the home of their family, the same restless spirit that led their ancestors up and down upon the earth has appeared to be always with them, it is only in a few rare cases that we find the son continuing to dwell where his father dwelt before him; and this fact, while affording another proof of the possession of common traits of character, has rendered it difficult to collect a complete genealogical record of the family.

The author began the work of collecting material for a family history some ten years since, and pursued it in such time as could be spared from the practice of his profession, but he soon found that another had been for a long time at work in the same field. The late Mead Allerton of Newark, Wayne County, New York, after working for many years at this task, left at his death a large and valuable manuscript, which was placed in the author's hands by his widow, and from which many details for this volume were obtained, especially in regard to the fourth, fifth and sixth generations of the Rhode Island and New York branches. Mead Allerton had not been able, however, to collect much information about the New Jersey branch, and to obtain this has been the most difficult part of the work, but the author believes that he is now able to present a complete genealogy of the entire family from 1585 to 1885. Where dates later than 1885 have been furnished, as in most cases they were, they have been given, but no attempt has been made to complete the genealogy of a date later than December 31 of that year.

The arrangement of the genealogy which has been used is believed to be the least confusing, and the one most easily followed in tracing descent or relationship. The different generations, counting Isaac of the Mayflower as the first, follow each other, and each member of the family is distinguished by two numbers; in the first place they are numbered consecutively from beginning to end, and when it becomes necessary to mention any member his or her number is always given, so that the reader can turn at once to the record; and every member is also distinguished by a number indicating the generation to which he belongs. Thus if any one wishes to trace Russell Allerton of Scituate, Rhode Island, he will find his name in the index, and turning to the proper page will find him thus numbered, "64 Russell^7," he will also find a record of his life and that he was the son of Roger^6 (31), and turning back to 31, he will find that Roger^6 was the son of John^5 (13), and thus he can trace his descent back to Isaac^4.

In order to keep the volume within the limits desired, it has been necessary to make the record of each family as brief as possible, and thus the author has been compelled to omit many details that were interesting and even valuable. No claim is made that perfection has been attained, the author is conscious of many defects, and no doubt errors will be found, but a strong effort has been made to exclude every fact that was not supported by apparently absolute evidence of its truth. Thus all details of the eighth, ninth and tenth generations have been obtained from living members of the family, and as far as possible they have been carefully revised and verified. And in preparing the record of the earlier generations much that appeared to be and no doubt was true has been rejected, because the evidence to absolutely confirm it was lacking; no credence has been given to common fame or tradition, and if the author has erred at all in this respect it has been on the side of strict requirement of proof, and in no case has conjecture or imagination been resorted to to fill a gap.

The name of Allerton is one that is comparatively common in some parts of England, and there are several families now in the United States who are in no way related to us, being emigrants from England themselves or the descendants of such, a list of these Allertons will be found at the end of the genealogical record. The beauty of the name has also caused it to be frequently used by novelists and other writers, and it has been occasionally assumed by persons not belonging to the family, some of whom have not been of a character calculated to reflect credit on any family.

Where nearly every one to whom the author has applied for information has gladly responded, it may seem unfair to mention any in particular, but while the author takes this opportunity to thank all who have in any manner assisted him, he feels that the members of the famlly generally ought to know the names of those who have rendered particular service. Besides Mead Allerton to whom the greatest credit is due for many years of patient and painstaking research, the author has received valuable assistance from the following persons:

Mrs. Jane G. Allerton, of Salem, Ohio.
James M. Allerton, of Port Jervis, New York.
Orville H. Allerton, of Newark, New York.
Mrs. Clara E. Delap, of Osnaburgh, Ohio.
Charles B. Allerton, of Keelersville, Michigan.
Ezekiel Allerton, of Roanoke, Indiana.
Lemira C. Allerton, of Youngstown, Ohio.
Mrs. James Kynett, of Alliance, Ohio.
Jasper Tilden, of Jefferson, Wisconsin.
H. D. Hutson, of Deerfield, Ohio.

In the matter of inserting portraits the only rule followed has been to give as many as possible, and a sincere endeavor has been made to make the portraits fairly representative of all the branches of the family, and of as many generations as possible. In justice to himself the author desires to say, that in giving a space to his own portrait, he has yielded to the request of a large proportion of the family. And in fact the desires of others have been carefully considered in many respects, and such changes in the plan or scope of the history have from time to time been made, as seemed likely to make it satisfactory to the great majority of those interested.

In conclusion the author earnestly requests all members of the family and all others into whose hands this volume may come, to carefully examine it, and if they find any errors or omissions of any kind, to notify him at once, as it is his intention to print in due time a sheet of additions and corrections, that will be sent to all having the history for insertion in the same.

At the end of the volume will be found a few sheets of blank paper upon which the record of each family can be continued, and it is hoped that this will be done in every case.

WALTER S. ALLERTON.

NEW YORK, Dec., 1888.

THE ALLERTON FAMILY.

In reviewing the history of the Allerton family the circumstance that first attracts our attention is the slow growth in numbers prior to 1800. The names of only eighty-three Allertons who were born before the opening of the present century are mentioned in this volume. This remarkably slow increase is accounted for by the fact, that Isaac the second, from whom the family is · descended, left but one son, Isaac the third; and he in his turn left but two sons, John and Jesse; and if Jesse had other sons than Zachariah they undoubtedly perished in the massacre of Wyoming.

Since 1800 however the family has rapidly increased in numbers, until at the present time there are at least three hundred persons living who are Allertons by birth and lineal descendants of Isaac of the Mayflower.

While they are scattered over the entire country, by far the greater number reside in the States of New York, Ohio and Michigan, while in New England, the original home of the Pilgrims, there are now less than a dozen members.

For convenience in tracing the history of the family the author at an early period of his work began to divide them into three branches; the Rhode Island branch, being the descendants of John[5]; the New York branch, being the descendants of Isaac[5]; and the New Jersey branch, being the descendants of Zachariah[5].

The Rhode Island branch is now practically extinct, there being but one male descendant of John[5] now living, Henry Allerton, of Lawrence, Massachusetts.

The New York and New Jersey branches are about equal in numbers, there being about seventy male representatives of each now living. The majority of the members of the New York branch are still residents of that State, while the New Jersey branch, though more widely scattered, seems to be more numerous in Ohio than in any other State.

The New York branch, which is entitled to the honor of being the older and principal branch of the family, has always been the most successful, and has contained the larger number of men who have attained to positions of eminence in professional or business life. Some curiosity has been shown in regard to the head of the family, and it is a fact of some interest that the late Mead Allerton of Newark, New York, who first began the collection of materials for a family history, was himself the head of the Allerton family, his descent from Isaac[2] being direct through the oldest sons in every generation. Who is entitled to claim the honor at present is a matter of some doubt perhaps, but the ordinary rule of succession would make his brother, Ransom Allerton, of Manchester, Ontario County, New York, the present head of the Allerton family in the United States.

The history of the Rhode Island branch is very brief; they resided in Rhode Island and in Windham County, Connecticut, and were generally farmers, but many of the sons of this family died young and unmarried, others inherited consumption from their mothers and died in youth or early manhood, until, as has been stated, the branch is now practically extinct.

The New York branch, after residing in Connecticut about fifty years, removed to Dutchess county, in New York, and to the county of Greene, on the west bank of the Hudson, where many of them reside to this day, and from there they gradually followed the general tendency of settlement to the west, and at the present time the most of them are to be found in central and western New York, while many have become residents of the north-western States.

The New Jersey branch has always shown a roving and unsettled disposition, their history has been the most varied and the most difficult to trace. It is certain that Jesse⁴ had at least two other sons besides Zachariah⁵, but no traces of any of their descendants have ever been found. There is a tradition, which seems to be entitled to acceptance, that two sons of Jesse, after removing to New Jersey with Zachariah, continued still further into the wilderness, and settling in the Wyoming valley, were killed with all their families at the time of the celebrated massacre. There is no mention of the name in any of the accounts of the massacre, but this is not conclusive proof that they were not there at the time, and in most accounts we find the names of several families of Athertons among the victims, and this we know to have been the most common of the many mistaken forms which the family name has often taken. It has been very difficult to obtain facts as to names, dates, etc., of the members of the New Jersey branch of the fifth, sixth and seventh generations, and the rule, which has been invariably adhered to, of rejecting every item about which there seemed to be even the suspicion of doubt, has rendered it impossible to give many details of their lives. But the chain of descent has been traced in every case with absolute certainty, so that every living member of the family can readily follow his own line back to the common ancestor, and can ascertain the exact degree of relationship existing between himself and any other Allerton. The sons and grandsons of Zachariah gradually drifted from New Jersey westward through Pennsylvania to north-eastern Ohio, where the greater number of his descendants now reside, although many of them are found in Michigan, Indiana and other western States.

The great majority of the family are to-day, as they have always been, farmers. They have never showed a tendency to city life, and very few are at present dwelling in any of our large cities. Outside of farming the occupation most favored has been that of machinist.

Each of the learned professions has had several representatives. The clergymen have been Reuben[7], Isaac[7] and Job D[9], of whom only the latter is now living. The physicians were Reuben[6], Cornelius[7], Goodwin[7] and Cornelius[8], all able and successful practitioners, but at present there are none living engaged in that profession.

The three lawyers are Russell[7], of Scituate, Rhode Island, who died in 1815, and James M[8], of Port Jervis, New York and Walter S.[9], of New York City, both of whom are now living.

Members of the family have fought in all the wars that have occurred since the landing of the Pilgrims, including the old Indian wars, the Revolution, the war of 1812, the Mexican war and the Rebellion. The history of the last war shows that besides several who aided the National government in civil capacities, many Allertons left their homes and went forth to battle and to die for the preservation of that liberty which their great ancestor had done so much to establish.

The Allerton family has as yet given no great names to history, they have never sought office or the rewards of political strife, the occupations to which they have generally devoted themselves have never been those that lead to fame or to political preferment, they have been farmers, merchants or mechanics, and have been content to be good citizens and honest men. There is no record of an Allerton having ever been convicted of a felony, and although there have been a few black sheep, the whole history of the family is remarkably free from moral blemishes of any kind.

Physically, they have always been a hardy and vigorous race, and in general long lived, many living to be ninety or more, and one, the late Samuel W. Allerton, of Newark, New York, being ninety-nine years and eight months old at his death. In appearance the majority are large framed, rather over than under middle height, fair complexioned with dark hair and eyes, many have brown or sandy hair and some blue or gray eyes, but few, if any, have been known who were of a distinctly blonde type. In youth they are generally slender and quick in action, and many have been noted for strength and dexterity, but they are apt to become quite fleshy in old age. The most prominent physical characteristic of the family is the shape of the forehead, eyes and nose, this can easily be seen by taking a number of portraits of members of all branches, and placing cards over them in such a manner as to show only the upper half of the face, when a remarkable similarity will be noticed by any one.

They are a quick tempered race and apt to act upon impulse, very decided in both likes and dislikes, and usually rather uncommunicative and reserved, not very ready to make new friends but firm in their attachment to old ones. Many of them have been called eccentric, and a few have been regarded, and perhaps justly, as carrying their erratic tendencies beyond a proper limit. In general they have intermarried with those who like themselves were descended from the early English settlers of this country, and the family has been kept remarkably free from any admixture of alien blood. There do not appear to be any diseases hereditary in the family, or any physical peculiarities other than those already mentioned.

In religion they are all Protestants and nearly all denominations are represented, but probably more belong to the Baptists than to any other one church.

In politics they are, with a very few exceptions, Republicans.

DAVID ALLERTON.
(129)

ISAAC ALLERTON.

THE exact time or place of Isaac Allerton's birth is not at present known to his descendants in the United States. He probably belonged to an old and honorable family of mixed Saxon and Danish descent, that had been for many centuries located in the south-eastern part of England, many representatives of which are still to be found in Suffolk and the adjacent counties. He was born between the years 1583 and 1585, and resided at London for some time prior to removing to Holland, in 1609.

Much speculation has been indulged in as to his business before that time, and he has been stated with confidence to have been a farmer, a seaman, a tailor, and more frequently has been more broadly called a merchant. One writer has shrewdly guessed that he had no particular business or occupation, which is quite possibly the more correct statement, since he could not have been more than twenty-four years old at the most when he left England.

He is generally admitted to have been the wealthiest of all the Pilgrims, and is one of the few among them to whom Bradford and other contemporaneous writers always give the prefix "Mr.," which in those days was used as an index of superior family or respectability. He was also one of the three upon whom the privilege of citizenship was conferred by the city of Leyden, his associates in this honor, which was given February 7, 1614, being William Bradford, afterwards Governor of the Plymouth colony, and Degory Priest, his brother-in-law. He was first married, as we learn from the records in the Staathuis or City Hall of Leyden, on November 4, 1611, to Mary Norris, of Newbury, in England, and at the sailing of the Pilgrims, he had four children, all born in Holland, three of whom, Bartholomew, Remember and Mary came over with their parents in the Mayflower, while the youngest, Sarah, remained behind and came over later with her aunt Sarah Priest.

On the 6th of September, 1620, the Mayflower sailed from Plymouth upon her memorable voyage, having on board, besides her officers and crew, one hundred and one passengers, and among them Isaac Allerton, with his wife and three children and one servant, John Hooke by name. The voyage, as was natural at that season of the year, was a long and stormy one, and disease and death were already at work among the over-crowded passengers of the little vessel, when on November 9, at break of day the sandy hills of Cape Cod became visible upon the western horizon. Their original design had been to make their settlement near the mouth of the Hudson, and accordingly they put about at once to the south, but soon found themselves entangled in the shoals of that dangerous coast, and being all of them, but especially the women and children, heartily sick of confinement within the narrow limits of the little vessel, the desire to be once more on land became too strong to be resisted. The captain also, having been bribed by the Dutch West India Company not to carry them to the Hudson, declared that further progress to the south was impossible and putting about once more to the north, they doubled the northern extremity of the Cape the next day, and came to anchor in Cape Cod harbor to ride out a storm.

This land, upon which they had now decided to settle, being in the forty-second degree of latitude, was without the territory of the Virginia Company, and therefore the charter they held became useless ; and some symptoms of faction and of an inclination

to throw off all authority appearing among the servants who had been hired in England, it was thought best by the leaders of the Colony that they should enter into an association for self government and bind themselves to be governed by the will of the majority. Accordingly after solemn prayer they drew up and signed the famous instrument which has ever since been known as the Compact, and which has most happily been styled the first of American Constitutions. It ran as follows: " In the
" name of God, Amen. We whose names are under-
" written; the loyal subjects of our dread sovereign
" lord King James, by the grace of God of Great
" Brittain, France and Ireland, King, Defender of
" the Faith, &c., having undertaken for the glory of
" God, and advancement of the Christian faith, and
" honour of our King and Country, a voyage to
" plant the first colony in the northern parts of
" Virginia; do by these presents solemnly and mutu-
" ally, in the presence of God and of one another,
" covenant and combine ourselves together into a
" civil body politic, for our better ordering and
" preservation, and furtherance of the ends aforesaid,
" and by virtue hereof to enact, constitute and frame
" such just and equal laws and ordinances, acts,
" constitutions and offices, from time to time, as shall

"be thought most meet and convenient for the gen-
"eral good of the Colony, unto which we promise
"all due obedience.

"In witness whereof we have hereunto subscribed
"our names at Cape Cod, the eleventh day of No-
"vember, in the year of the reign of our sovereign
"lord King James of England, France and Ireland,
"the eighteenth, and of Scotland the fifty-fourth.
"Anno Domini, 1620."

Isaac Allerton was the fifth signer of the compact, the only names which precede his being those of Carver, Bradford, Winslow and Brewster. They remained at anchor in Cape Cod Harbor for five weeks, during which time the men made many excursions to explore the surrounding country, while the women were taken on shore to wash the clothing. Finally, having selected a place for their settlement, on the 21st day of December, 1620, a date which by their act has been rendered one of the landmarks of history, they landed at Plymouth, and at once set about the erection of a store-house for their goods, and dwellings for themselves. But even before their landing several of their number had died, and although the winter proved to be an unusually mild one, it was still far more severe than those to which they had been accustomed, and this together with their enfeebled condition after the confinement of the voyage and the want of proper food and shelter, caused such sickness among the colonists that at times there were no more than six or seven of them well enough to nurse the sick, and by the coming of April, forty-four, or nearly one-half had died, and among them were Carver, the first governor, and his wife, and Mary the wife of Isaac Allerton, who died February 25th, 1621. While on the Mayflower in the harbor of Cape Cod, she had been delivered of a child, still-born, and the hardships and privations of that terrible winter proved too much for her strength thus enfeebled.

The first entry in the records of the Plymouth Colony is an incomplete list of "The Meersteads and Garden Plottes" assigned to those who came out on the Mayflower, at the first division of land. Each of these "Garden Plottes" contained one "aker." The list and diagram is as follows.

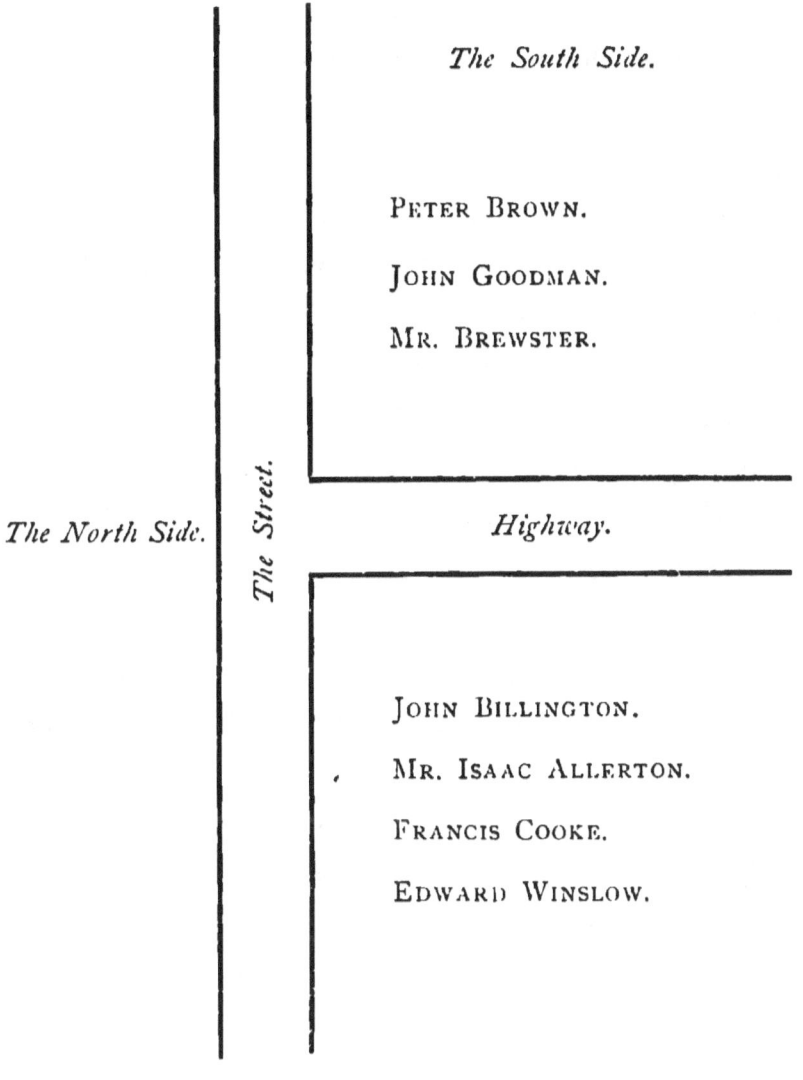

It will be noticed that the honorable prefix "Mr." is here given to Brewster and Allerton only.

The Street is now called Leyden street and leads from the harbor westward.

It is probable that Isaac Allerton built a house on his "Garden Plotte," but if he did he did not occupy it during the entire period of his residence in Plymouth, for in 1635, he lived at Rocky Nook, on Jones' River in Kingston, in a house which he afterwards sold "to my well beloved sonne-in-law Thomas Cushman," the location of which is still pointed out near the celebrated Elder's spring.

In March the colonists had grave apprehension of trouble with the Indians. On the night of the twenty-second an attack was expected and watch was kept, but there was no appearance of hostility, and as the old chronicle says, "The next day, Friday, "Captain Standish and Mr. Allerton went venturously "to visit King Massasoit, and were received by him "after his manner. He gave them 3 or 4 ground "nuts and some tobacco."

As the result of this visit a treaty of peace was concluded, which held good for more than fifty years.

In April, Governor Carver died, and William Bradford was then chosen Governor, and Isaac

Allerton Assistant Governor, a position which he held until 1624, and probably longer.

In September, 1621, a party of ten, including Isaac Allerton, went by water to explore what is now the harbor of Boston, and to visit the Indians who lived in that vicinity, and on this trip the first headland at Nantasket, at the entrance to the harbor was called Point Allerton, a name which it still retains, although it has sometimes been spelled Alderton; an adjoining hill in the town of Hull was also known for many years as Allerton Hill. For several years after the landing of the colonists Isaac Allerton was engaged, as were all the rest, in building houses and barns for shelter, in clearing and tilling the soil, and in managing with the other leading men, the affairs of the little settlement. We find him participating in another division of land in the spring of 1624, when seven acres, "on the south side of the Brook to the Baywards," were set off for him.

In 1626, he married Fear Brewster, the daughter of Elder William Brewster, who had come over in the ship Ann with her sister Patience, in 1623. She was a woman of a pleasing appearance and of a pious disposition, as we are told, and she is interesting to us as being the mother of that Isaac

Allerton, the second of the name, from whom the Allerton family is descended, She died in 1634.

In the fall of 1626, Isaac Allerton was sent by the colonists to England, to obtain certain supplies for them of which they were in great need, and to arrange if possible a composition with the Adventurers, as those men who had advanced the funds for the colony were called. Bradford says that he was selected as the agent of the colonists in this matter as "being well qualified by education and experience, and having the confidence of the Merchants of London," and these advantages of education and experience in the affairs of the world, enabled him to manage the affairs of the colony with signal success for a time, but beyond doubt they were the natural causes of the disagreements which afterward took place.

In the spring of 1627 he returned with the draft of a composition, "drawn by the best counsel of law they could get to make it firm." By this contract, which was dated at London, November 15, 1626, the Adventurers sold to the Colony their entire interest in the settlement for £1800, "to be "paid at the Royal Exchange, at London, every "Michaelmas, in nine annual installments of £200, "each," and it was provided that they were to forfeit thirty shillings per week, for every week the debt was not paid after it was due. This composition was unanimously sanctioned, and Isaac Allerton was at once sent back to England with full authority to ratify and confirm it.

At the same time the entire trade of the colony for a period of six years, was bound to William Bradford, Edward Winslow, Isaac Allerton, and several others, in consideration of their assuming the entire indebtedness, amounting in all to about £2400, and in addition they were to pay the colony £50 per annum in hoes and shoes.

Having satisfactorily arranged the composition with the Adventurers and paid them their first installment of £200, and having paid other debts, Isaac Allerton returned to Plymouth in the spring of 1628, bringing with him a supply of goods, and also a patent for a trading station on the Kennebec, but when they came to compare the patent with the region to which it applied, they found it "so strait and ill bounded," that he was again sent to England, for the third time, to obtain the enlargement and correction of this patent, and also a new patent for Plymouth, and to arrange for the removal of the remainder of the church at Leyden. He was compelled to return to Plymouth without accomplishing all he had been desired to do, but being immediately sent back again, in August, 1629, he had better success, and obtained the desired patent January 29, 1630. He went to England several times after this on business for the colonists or for himself, crossing the ocean in all seven times.

About this time, 1630, began his trouble with the colonists, or rather with Governor Bradford, the true cause of which it is difficult to ascertain, and with a full account of which I shall not weary the reader. Bradford's version can be found, written with all the energy and rancour of his narrow and prejudiced mind, in the pages of his famous journal, but it is a series of complaints rather than a statement of facts, and evidently fails to state the true grounds of the disagreement. We might offset the complainings of Bradford with the statements of those who were better able to know the true value of Isaac Allerton's services to the colony; thus James Sherley, one of the Adventurers and a steadfast friend of the colonists, writes, March 8, 1629, "He hath been a truly honest "friend to you all, either there or here. And if "any do, as I know some of them are apt to speak "ill of him, believe them not." And again on March 19, 1629, he writes, in a letter signed also by Timothy Hatherly, a friend of the colonists at London, " But the Lord so blessed his labours " (even beyond expectation in these evil days), as " he obtained the love and favor of great men in " repute and place, he got granted all Mr. Winslow " desired in his letters to me and more also." Many similar statements might be quoted from letters and writings of other friends to the colony in England, while on the other hand Bradford complains bitterly that too much money had been expended in obtaining a charter, and that he had sometimes endeavored to further his own interests rather than those of the colony. But those who care to examine into the merits will inevitably come to the conclusion reached by a painstaking and impartial historian, that "As an agent Mr. " Allerton appears to have been indefatigable in his " attempts to promote the interests of his employers. " He was a person of uncommon activity, address " and enterprise."

The true cause however of this difficulty with the colonists and with Bradford in particular, is undoubtedly to be found in the fact, that he was in mind, education and practice far more liberal than they, and that while his associations in England with the merchants of London, and the officers of the court and government tended to still further broaden and liberalize his views, their seclusion in the forests and among the dangers of the little settlement at Plymouth was most admirably calculated to make still narrower and more bigoted natures that were already inclined to the most puritanical of views.

We know that the church at Leyden took offence at the liberal tendencies of Isaac Allerton, that the colonists were greatly offended at his apparently innocent mistake in employing the notorious Morton of Merry Mount as his secretary, although in these days, Morton would almost pass for a saint, and when he became known as a firm friend of Roger Williams, and was found to have sheltered and protected many of the oppressed and persecuted Quakers, the cup of his iniquity was indeed full to the minds of the colonists, and we are not surprised to hear that about 1636, he left Massachusetts in consequence of the religious intolerance of the people, and went to New Amsterdam to live. Like most of his descendants, Isaac Allerton, though a just and fair minded man, was of a quick temper, apt to resent an affront, and impetuous in acting upon his impulses, and therefore, when once a difference had arisen between him and a majority of the Plymouth colonists, who were no doubt well represented by their narrow and dogmatic governor, there was little possibility of any reconciliation, even had there been more in common in their natures and their ways of life and thought.

Moreover he had given great offence by embarking extensively in business which conflicted in many ways with the industries of the colony. He was admittedly the first merchant of New England, and the founder of the coasting trade and the fishing industry. We find early mention of vessels owned by him, and he was the first to welcome Winthrop and his Company to the shores of the New World. Winthrop says in his journal, under date of June 12, 1630, "About four in the morning we were "near our port, we shot off two pieces of ordinance "and sent our skiff to Mr. Pierce (which lay in "the harbor and had been there———days before); "about an hour after Mr. Allerton came on board "us in a shallop as he was sailing to Pemaquid." In 1632 he attempted to set up a rival trading station on the Kennebec, and also to establish one on the Penobscot, but both these enterprises were unsuccessful, the latter station being broken up by the French in 1634. In 1633, Winthrop records that he fished with light boats at Marble Harbor, and he is justly regarded as the founder of Marblehead, for he made that place the headquarters of his fishing fleet, built a large warehouse, and resided there a great part of the time with his son-in-law Moses Maverick, until his liberal views again brought him into trouble with the General Court, as they had previously done with his old associates at Plymouth, and he was given "leave to depart from Marblehead."

That he was liberal in other matters as well as in religion, we know from the following extract from the records, under date of December 2, 1633: " Whereas Mr. Will. Bradford was appointed in the " behalf of the Court to enter upon the estate of " Godbert Godbertson and Zarah his wife, and to " discharge the debts of the said Godbert so far " as his estate will make good. And whereas the " greatest part of his debts are owing to Mr. " Isaack Allerton of Plym., Mercht., late brother of " the said Zarah. The said Isaack hath given leave " to all other his creditors to be fully discharged " before he receives any thing of his particular debts " to himself, desiring rather to lose all than other " men should lose any."

But about this time misfortunes began to come thick and heavy upon him. In 1634 his trading house at Machias was taken by the French and Indians and destroyed by fire with all its contents. In February of the same year, " Mr. Cradock's " house at Marblehead was burnt down about " midnight, there being in it Mr. Allerton and many " fishermen whom he employed that season." The same year, returning from a trading voyage to Port Royal, " his pinace was cast away and entirely lost;" and on December 12, 1634, his wife died at Plymouth.

In 1635 his misfortunes still continued. In March, he was notified to leave Marblehead on account of his religious views, and in May he transferred all his houses, buildings and stages for curing fish at that place to his son-in-law, Moses Maverick. In August, a bark belonging to him, which had been hired to transport Rev. Mr. Avery and his family, from Newbury to Marblehead, was lost at Cape Anne, and twenty-one persons perished, and in 1636, while returning from Penobscot, he was himself shipwrecked.

From 1636 to 1646, he resided most of the time at New Amsterdam, where he was engaged in the coasting and tobacco trades, having a warehouse on the East River, somewhere near where the foot of Maiden Lane now is. That his intelligence and enterprise were thoroughly appreciated by the Dutch settlers is shown by the circumstance, that when, in 1643, a Council of eight were chosen from among the citizens, nominally to assist Governor Kieft, but in reality to manage him, Isaac Allerton was one of the number. While living at New Amsterdam, however, he made many voyages to Virginia and even to the West Indies, and frequently visited the New England Colonies; and notwithstanding the treatment he had received he often rendered good service to such residents of the Massachusetts settlement as came in his way. Thus Winthrop writes, in 1643: "Three ministers which " were sent to Virginia were wrecked on Long Island; " Mr. Allerton, of New Haven, being there took " great pains and care of them, and procured them " a very good pinace and all things necessary."

And in a letter from one John Haynes to Governor Winthrop, it is stated, "There is late news by " a vessel that came to the Dutch and from thence " to New Haven, by Mr. Allerton. The substance " thus: that there has been a great battle between " the King and Parliament forces."

In 1644, he was wrecked at Scituate, on his way from New Haven to the Colonies, and at this time we find the first mention of his third wife. The date of this marriage is not known nor the surname and residence of his wife; her first name was Johanna, and he is generally thought to have married her at New Haven, but I am inclined to think that she came more probably from Marblehead or Salem. She appears to have been a woman of a most excellent character, and she outlived her husband many years. At the time of this marriage Isaac Allerton must have been nearly sixty years of age and the union proved to be a childless one.

About 1647, Isaac Allerton became a permanent resident of New Haven, and at that place he lived the remainder of his life, although making occasional trips to New Amsterdam and Massachusetts. He built himself a "grand house on the Creek with Four Porches," on a home lot of two acres, which was situated about where Union street now is, just south of Cherry street.

An old plan of New Haven in 1748, shows the house of Simon Eyres, a descendent of his in this location, and mentions Isaac Allerton as the original owner. When he lived there the house stood on a gentle declivity sloping down to the harbor in front and to the creek on the west, affording a view of the waters of the Sound even to the coast of Long Island, and it must have been just such a home as would be most pleasant for the last years of one who had been so long a follower of the seas.

We find many mentions of Captain Isaac Allerton, as he is there called, in the old records of New Haven.

On March 10, 1647, the names of the people as they were seated in the meeting house were put upon record, and we find "Thomas Nash, Mr. Allerton and Bro. Perry," assigned to "the second seat of the cross seats at the end." It is to be noticed that as usual he is here given the honorable prefix "Mr."

The following account of a little difficulty which Mrs. Allerton had with the officials of the town, during her husband's absence upon one of his voyages, shows that human nature, especially as it develops itself in petty officers, was the same then as now. At a Court held at New Haven, August 6, 1650, "Mr Allerton's fence was complained of. " Jno. Cooper and the Marshall informed the Court " that Mrs. Allerton hath had notice of it three " times and yet the fence is not mended, but two " places remain defective as John Cooper says." The Court ordered that Mr. Allerton pay two shillings for the two defective places, each time they have so warned. The fence does not appear to have been mended, for the same report is repeated from one court to another, and an additional fine of two shillings ordered each time, until December, when "Mr. Evans saith Mrs. Allerton desired him to "acquaint the Court with the case." The explanation being that there had been a long misunderstanding between her and John Cooper about the location of the fence complained of. The Court said they "must rest on John Cooper's report be-"cause he is in a public trust in this matter of "fence, and therefore it is ordered that Mrs. Allerton "pay for the two defects, two shillings."

The misfortunes which had pressed so thickly upon him during the last years of his residence in Massachusetts, as to gain for him the name of the "unlucky," do not appear to have entirely deserted him yet, for we find the following record under date of November 2, 1652: "Robert Paine "and William Meaker were complained of for absence "from training. The Court was informed that Mr. "Allerton that morning sent to Goodyears to get "them free because of some urgent occasion about "his vessel. The Court considering that he did "send to ask leave, and it was upon that occasion, "and the time the vessel hath lain, and the afflicted "state of Mr. Allerton otherwise, did for this time "pass it over without a fine."

Isaac Allerton was now approaching the threescore years and ten, which are the generally accepted limit of human existence; his life had been one of hardship, activity and exposure; his son Isaac was now grown to manhood, and able to manage in great part the extensive, although not very successful business in which he had been so long engaged, and for the last few years of his life he seems to have resided most of the time quietly in his house upon the Bay.

He died about the beginning of the year 1659, being then in all probability nearly seventy-five years old. He was undoubtedly buried in the old Burying Ground at New Haven, occupying the square in the very heart of the present city, upon which stands the old State House and three churches. No monument or grave-stone has ever been found, nor is there any record of one being among those that were removed to the new Cemetery. At that time grave-stones were not made in this country, and the trouble and expense of importing them was so great that but few of durable material were used. But there can be little or no doubt that the dust of one of the Pilgrim Fathers reposes beneath the Elms of New Haven's public square. An Inventory of his estate, taken February 12,

1659, was presented to the Court April 5, 1659. "Mrs. Allerton being asked if there was any Will "by her husband, answered there was, but she "thought her son had it with him, who was now "gone from home." On July 5, his son, having returned, presented the Will, but the estate being badly insolvent the business was referred to the Court of Magistrates in October. At that Court the writing presented as the last Will and Testament of Isaac Allerton, although informal and without date, was sworn to by John Harriman and Edward Preston, the subscribing witnesses, as sealed and subscribed by Mr. Allerton deceased, "whilst he "had the use of his understanding and memory in "a competent degree."

This Will was little else than a few memoranda of debts due to him, which he desired his son Isaac and his wife to receive and pay out to his creditors as far as they would go, and it is only valuable to us as showing the nature and the extent of his business. It begins thus, "An account "of the debts due at the Dutch," meaning at New Amsterdam.

Among the debts are, "700 guilders by Tho. "Hall by arbitration of Captain Willett and Augustus "Harman, about Captain Scarlet which I paid "out;" "900 guilders from John Peterson the Bore, "as by George Woolseys book will appear." One item which helps us to fix the date of this Will approximately is a memorandum of a sum owing him from Henry Brassen, for rent for eighteen months from October 1656, to the last of May 1658, for three rooms for 3 guilders a week. After the clause constituting his son and wife trustees, he adds, as if it was an after-thought, a memorandum of "a parcel of book lace in Captain Willett's hands 1300 and odd Guilders." Next to this is the place of the seal, and it concludes with these two sentences: " My Brother Brewster owes me four " score pounds and odd, as the obligations appear." " Besides all my debts in Delaware Bay and Vir- " ginia, which in my books will appear, and in " Barbadoes what he can get."

ISAAC ALLERTON, Senior."

His son, Isaac Allerton the second, purchased from the creditors his father's dwelling house, orchard and barn, with two acres of meadow, and gave it to his step-mother for use during her life. She occupied it until her death in 1682, when it passed to Mrs. Eyres, the daughter of Isaac the second, and it was finally torn down in 1740.

It was in this house that the regicide Judges Whalley and Goffe found temporary shelter and concealment in 1661. Stiles, in his History of the Regicide Judges, says that they were protected by Mrs. Eyres, but in this he is in error, for, having been born in 1653, she was but eight years old at the time.

It was Mrs. Johanna Allerton, the widow of Isaac Allerton of the Mayflower, and her daughter-in-law, Elizabeth Allerton, who received and sheltered the judges.

No portrait of Isaac Allerton has come down to us, but he is said to have been slightly above the average height, of a spare but muscular frame, with dark hair and beard, a clear complexion and strongly marked features, a good looking rather than a handsome man. In the great majority of his descendants there can be noticed a great similarity of development in the upper portion of the head and face, more especially noticeable in the forehead, eyes and nose, and there can be no doubt that these physical marks, together with certain well defined traits of character, have descended to us from our common ancestor. He was superior to all of his associates on the Mayflower, except possibly Winslow, and one or two others, in education, and superior to all of them in knowledge of the world and familiarity with business, and as his experience in these matters was so much greater, his mental horizon was far wider and his views more liberal and more tolerant of the opinions of others. The only wonder is that he was able to agree with them as long as he did. The services which he rendered to the Colony have been fully appreciated by a few careful historians only; poetry and romance have combined to spread the fame of Standish the soldier, or of Alden the clerk, while the record of Allerton's work is buried in the dusty recesses of English offices, but had there been no Standish among the Colonists there could have been found others as competent to battle with the Indians, while it is hardly possible that any man among them could have accomplished all that Isaac Allerton did in London, and it is not too much to say that the very existence of the Plymouth Colony depended for a time upon the success of his negotiations there.

For two centuries and a third the dust of the Pilgrim leader has slumbered beneath the elms of New Haven, but his memory is fresh to-day and will always endure, not only in the hearts of his descendants but in common with his heroic companions of the Mayflower, his name will be forever cherished by the entire people of that mighty nation, the corner-stone of whose foundations was so deeply and so enduringly laid by the Pilgrims of Plymouth.

THE SECOND GENERATION.

1. ISAAC ALLERTON, of the Mayflower, had five children.
2. I. BARTHOLOMEW^2, by his first wife Mary Norris, of Newbury, in England, born in Holland about 1612; he came over on the Mayflower with his parents, and was a resident of Plymouth in 1627, at the division among the settlers of the cattle brought from England, but shortly afterwards he accompanied his father to London, where he married and had children, but he never returned to America, and so far as is known no descendant of his has ever been found in this country.
3. II. REMEMBER^2, also by his first wife Mary Norris, born in Holland in 1614; she also came over in the Mayflower, and was living in 1627, but probably died soon after, unmarried.

Gov. Bradford says that she married Moses Maverick of Salem, but he has confounded her with her younger sister Sarah.

4. III. MARY^2, also by his first wife, born in Holland in June, 1616, came over in the Mayflower; was married in 1636 to Thomas Cushman, and from this marriage came the Cushman family of Massachusetts. She died in 1699, the last survivor of the Pilgrims of the Mayflower.

5. IV. SARAH^2, also by his first wife, born in Holland in January, 1618; she did not come over in the Mayflower with her parents, but followed them soon after in the care of her aunt Sarah, the wife of Degory Priest, who afterwards married Mr. Godbertson. She married, in 1637, Moses Maverick, of Marblehead, had a large family of children, and died about 1655 or 1656.

6. V. ISAAC^2, from whom the Allerton family is descended, was the son of Isaac^1 by his second wife, Fear Brewster; he was born in Plymouth, in 1630, and graduated from Harvard College in 1650. He accompanied his father after that on his voyages

between Plymouth, New Haven and New Amsterdam, and was associated with him in the coasting business. After his father's death in 1659, he purchased from the creditors of his estate, the dwelling-house, orchard and barn, with two acres of meadow, and in the New Haven Records we find a deed recorded, dated October 4th, 1660, by which he conveys to his " Mother-"in-law, Mrs. Johanna Allerton, the house " that she now dwells in at New Haven, " with all the furniture in it and the lands " and appurtenances belonging to it, to " hold and enjoy during the term of her " life, and afterward to return into the " possession of his daughter Elizabeth " Allerton and her heirs, and in case of " her dyeing without issue, then to return " to him the first donor, and his heirs and " executors without intermission."

To this deed after it was recorded was added on the margin of the book the following " true record " of a postscript, " This deed, though never witnessed when " granted, I do hereby confirm to all " intents and purposes as if it had been

"authentically witnessed, and so sign and
"seal the same in presence of

     JOHN SALMON,
"March 10. WILLIAM CORFIELD.
"1682-3.   ISAAC ALLERTON."

During the period intervening between the execution of this deed in 1660, and the confirmation in 1683, he resided most if not all of the time, in Northumberland County, Virginia, where a daughter of his married Hancock Lee, seventh son of Col. Richard Lee.

His business took him upon frequent voyages, upon one of which he is said to have visited England, and while upon a voyage to the West Indies about the year 1690, he is generally believed to have died and been buried at sea, and it is said that his son-in-law, Simon Eyres, who was associated with him in business, died at the same time. He was married probably in 1652, but little is known of his wife except that her first name was Elizabeth. He was a man of enterprise and ability and generally successful in business, but from boyhood a wanderer upon sea and land, having no settled habitation and consequently leaving but few records of his life for the information of his descendants.

Besides these Isaac[1] had at least two other children, both of whom, however, died in infancy.

SAMUEL W. ALLERTON.
(60)

THE THIRD GENERATION.

ISAAC² (6) had three children.

7. I. ELIZABETH³, born at New Haven, September 27, 1653. She married for her first husband, December 23, 1675, Benjamin Starr, who died in 1678, leaving one child, Allerton Starr, born January 6, 1677. For her second husband, she married, July 22, 1679, Simon Eyres or Heyres, a sea captain, by whom she had several children.

8. II. ISAAC³, born at New Haven, June 11, 1655. He accompanied his father to Virginia when a child, but returned to New Haven about 1683, and resided there, and at Norwich in the same State, during the remainder of his life, following his son, John⁴, to Coventry, Rhode Island, shortly before his death, the exact date of which is not known. He was a farmer and also a dealer in the products of the country, a quiet business man, taking but little part in public affairs, but serving with credit in the Indian wars.

But few details of his life have come down to us; the name of his wife is not definitely known, nor can we say with any certainty how many children he had. Besides John[4] and Jesse[4], who grew to manhood, married and left descendants, he undoubtedly had another son, Isaac, who died young and unmarried, as well as several daughters.

9. III. A Daughter, whose name is at present unknown, as well as the date of her birth, although it was not far from 1660. She married Hancock Lee, the son of Col. Richard Lee, of Virginia.

THE FOURTH GENERATION.

ISAAC³ (8) had children as follows:

10. I. JOHN⁴, born at New Haven about 1685. In early manhood he removed to Norwich with his parents, and from there he went to Coventry in Rhode Island, where he had a farm and also dealt largely in produce, and was widely known as an energetic business man; but like his father he lived quietly and left but few records for the information of his descendants. He had a large family, and his wife, whose maiden name is unknown, survived him many years, and removed with a daughter, who married a man named Sweet, to the State of New York. He died at Coventry about the middle of the eighteenth century.

11. II. JESSE⁴, born at New Haven, in 1686 or 1687. In him the roving disposition of the family, which had been dormant for two generations, re-asserts itself, and it has ever been a prominent characteristic of his

descendants. He married in early life and lived in various parts of Connecticut and Massachusetts; one account states that he died in the latter, while another states that he went to New Jersey with his son Zachariah and died there at an advanced age. He undoubtedly had a comparatively large family, but of his daughters absolutely nothing is known, and indeed no attempt has been made to trace the female members of the fourth and fifth generations. The tradition that several of his sons were victims of the Wyoming massacre is given elsewhere in this volume.

12.   III. Isaac[4], born at New Haven, about 1690. Died young and unmarried.

THE FIFTH GENERATION.

John[4] (10) had eight children.

13. 1. Isaac[5], born at Norwich, Connecticut, in 1724. But little is known with certainty of his early years, but after his marriage to Lucy Spaulding, about 1745, he lived at Canterbury and Plainfield, and followed the business of builder as well as being a farmer. In appearance he was a tall and robust man, and had considerable local fame as an athlete, until he sustained an injury to one of his legs while building a bridge, from the effects of which he never entirely recovered. Prior to the War of the Revolution he was quite wealthy, but having shown his devotion to the continental cause by taking the paper money of the provinces in exchange for produce and supplies furnished to the troops to a large amount, he eventually lost the greater part of his property. He removed to Amenia, in Dutchess County, New York, in 1792, and died there December 26, 1807.

During his lifetime he possessed several mementoes of the Mayflower and of the earlier years of the Plymouth Colony, among others a broad-axe which had been used to hew the timbers for the first house built by the Colonists, and a fuzee-gun taken in battle from an Indian warrior, but unfortunately since his death these relics have been lost. His wife survived him and died in 1813, aged 86 years, and they are both buried in the Cemetery at Amenia.

14. II. JOHN[5], born at Norwich, Connecticut, about 1728. He was a farmer and also a cooper. He resided at Coventry, Rhode Island, where he married a widow named Rose Cooper, whose maiden name was Burlingame, by whom he had eight children. He injured one of his fingers while placing a back-log upon an old fashioned wood fire, from which blood poisoning resulted, and he died at the age of 48 years. He was buried in the family grave-yard on his farm at Coventry.

15. III. ELIZABETH[5], born at Norwich, in 1730, died young.

16. IV. ESTHER[5], born at Norwich, in 1733.

17. V. MARY[5], born at Norwich, in 1736.

18. VI. A Son⁵, born at Norwich, in 1739, died in infancy.
19. VII. Anna⁵, born at Norwich, in 1742.
20. VIII. Sarah⁵, born at Norwich, in 1746.

Jesse⁴ (11) had one child, besides others of whom we have no record.

21. I. Zachariah⁵, born in Massachusetts, about 1730, he removed to New Jersey, and was twice married; by his first wife he had several daughters, of whom nothing is known, and by his second wife six sons and one daughter. It is said that he went to Northumberland County, Pennsylvania, after the close of the Revolutionary War, in which he served in the Continental Army, and died there about the year 1800.

THE SIXTH GENERATION.

ISAAC⁵ (13) had six children.

22. I. JONATHAN⁶, born at Plainfield, Connecticut, September 15, 1746. His early life was passed on his father's farm, where he obtained a practical knowledge of farming as there practiced, and also of his father's trade of builder and house joiner. He also taught school in winter, and for several years he was so engaged at Amenia, in Dutchess County, New York, where, September 17, 1772, he married Bathsheba Mead, daughter of Joshua Mead. He was well educated for those days and an excellent penman, being much in demand to draw contracts, deeds, and similar papers. He served in the War of the Revolution until compelled by sickness to return home, and evidently shared in his father's confidence in the Continental currency, for we are told that he sold his interest and that of his mother-in-law, in the homestead farm for $2,000, and took

his pay in that money, by which he lost nearly his entire property. In 1783, in company with others of his fellow townsmen, he purchased a tract of land, known as the Van Schaick patent, in the town of Cairo, in Greene County, New York, and removed there with his family. Here he taught school for several winters, and after filling a prominent place in the affairs of the little settlement for many years, he died August 10, 1806. His wife survived him for a long time, and died July 4, 1838, aged 84 years, and was buried beside him in the family grave-yard on the farm.

23. II. DAVID[6], born at Canterbury, Connecticut, February 14, 1750. He was a farmer all his life, a man of a strong religious temperament and a most kindly disposition. He resided until manhood at Canterbury, where he was married about 1775, to Janet Montgomery, of Rhode Island, a relative of General Richard Montgomery. About the year 1785 he removed to Amenia, Dutchess County, New York, where he resided about ten years, and then moved again to Madison County, residing successively at Sangerfield,

Smithville and Hamilton, at which latter place he died, October 31, 1828. His wife, by whom he had a large family, died, September 17, 1830, aged 71 years.

24. III. REUBEN[6], born at Canterbury, Connecticut, December 25, 1753. He was unusually well educated for those times, and studied medicine with Dr. Fitch of New Haven, and surgery with Dr. Spaulding of Norwich, a relative of his mother, and became eminent as a physician and surgeon. He resided at Amenia, Dutchess County, New York, and during the War of the Revolution he served as a Surgeon in the Army of the Colonies, in which capacity he was present at the battle of Saratoga, and the surrender of Burgoyne. He married, September 1, 1779, Lois Atherton, of New Hampshire, and died at Amenia, October 13, 1808.

25. IV. ANNA[6], born at Canterbury, April 20, 1757. Married in 1777, David Ransom, and in 1812, went with him to Herkimer County, New York, were she died, April 26, 1853.

26. V. ALICE[6], born at Windham, Connecticut, May 23, 1765. Married late in life, David Runnels, and died in 1852, without issue.

27. VI. SARAH[6], born at Plainfield, Connecticut, February 12, 1770. Married George James, a farmer of Rhode Island, by whom she had several children, and with whom she removed to Dutchess County, New York, where she died in August, 1858, the last descendant of the Allertons of the sixth generation. Many details for this genealogy were obtained from her.

JOHN[5] (14) had eight children.

28. I. FREELOVE[6], born at Coventry, Rhode Island, in 1753. Married a Mr. Albro, of Saratoga County, New York.
29. II. SARAH[6], born at Coventry, Rhode Island, in 1755. Died unmarried in 1837.
30. III. JERUSHA[6], born at Coventry, Rhode Island, in 1760. Died unmarried in 1798.
31. IV. ROGER[6], born at Coventry, Rhode Island, in 1763. He was well educated and taught school for several years in early manhood. In 1788, he married Mrs. Elsie Phillips, a widow, and daughter of Lieutenant Governor West, of Scituate, Rhode Island; prior to his wife's death, in 1828, he was a farmer at Scituate, and afterwards he kept a tavern

at Providence for many years. He died in 1849, and was buried at Coventry, beside his parents.

32. V. John[6], born at Coventry, February 13, 1765. He resided in youth for several years with his uncle Isaac[5], in Plainfield, Connecticut, and when about 16 years old moved to Brooklyn in the same State, where, in 1810, he married Molly Barrett. He was an industrious and successful farmer, and died at Brooklyn, January 2, 1839. His wife had previously died, July 3, 1838.

33. VI. Betsey[6], born at Coventry, in 1767. She accompanied her sister Freelove to Saratoga, and married Samuel Campbell, by whom she had several children.

34. VII. Russell[6], born at Coventry, in 1769. He also removed to Saratoga County, New York, where he died, unmarried, in 1800.

35. VIII. Rose Anne[6], born at Coventry, in 1771. Died, unmarried, at Coventry, in 1836.

Zachariah[5] (21) had seven children by his last wife.

36. I. Amos[6], born in New Jersey, April 6, 1760. He was by occupation a tanner and manu-

facturer of boots and shoes, and also at times a farmer, and of an unstable nature, never residing long in one locality. He married in early life, Chloe Stiles, and had a large family, and died at Lake Mills, Wisconsin, September 15, 1846.

37. II. JOHN[6], born in New Jersey, March 10, 1763. He was a farmer and a successful business man; he was married four times, by his first wife he had two children, and by his second wife, Rachel Crage, he had six children. He resided in Crawford County, Pennsylvania, until after the birth of his children, when he removed to Ohio, and resided at Waynesburgh and Smithtown. He died at the latter place, April 8, 1851.

38. III. STEPHEN[6], born in New Jersey, September 21, 1767. Married, about 1795, Catharine Lutz. He was a farmer by occupation, and resided in Northumberland County, Pennsylvania, and afterwards at Coitsville, Mahoning County, Ohio, where he died November 15, 1832.

39. IV. SAMUEL[6], born in New Jersey, about 1767. He left home in early manhood, and as nothing has ever been heard of him or his

descendants, is supposed to have died young and unmarried.

40. V. Job[6], born in New Jersey, about 1770. He was a machinist by occupation, and resided in New Jersey and at Baltimore and Harper's Ferry, and finally settled in Stark County, Ohio. He married while young, Grace ——, and had a large family, of whom only four lived. He died in Stark County, about 1840.

41. VI. Jesse[6], born in New Jersey, about 1773. Died, unmarried, at the age of eighteen.

42. VII. Hannah[6], born in New Jersey, about 1775.

THE SEVENTH GENERATION.

JONATHAN⁶ (22) had seven children.

43. I. JOSHUA⁷, born at Amenia, Dutchess County, New York, November 7, 1776. He was taken by his parents to Greene County in childhood, where he resided during the remainder of his life. He was a farmer by occupation, and being by nature both industrious and intelligent, he was unusually successful and acquired considerable property during a long and upright life. He married, April 29, 1804, Polly Bassett, then 24 years old, and like himself a descendant of the Pilgrims, by whom he had a large family. He died at Cairo, in Greene County, September 14, 1862.

44. II. ISAAC⁷, born at Amenia, January 15, 1779. He resided with his grand parents, after his father's removal to Greene County, in 1783, until he was 15 years old, when he followed him there and assisted him upon his farm until his marriage, March

6, 1806, to Charlotte Townsend. After his marriage he became a wagon maker, and after some years a miller, but being unsuccessful in this latter venture, he removed in 1820, to Benton, in Yates County, and became a farmer, first in that vicinity, and afterwards at Prattsburgh, in Steuben County. He died at Savona, in that County, April 2, 1863.

45. III. John[7], born at Amenia, July 24, 1781. He accompanied his parents to Greene County while a child, and in 1808 he married Polly Andress and removed to Delaware County. He was a farmer, but was unsuccessful, and finally became insane and committed suicide in 1819.

46. IV. Sarah[7], born at Amenia, March 22, 1783. Died at Cairo, Greene Co., March 11, 1794.

47. V. Anna[7], born at Cairo, Greene County, December 13, 1785. Married Reuben German, February 10, 1816, and died at Cairo, July 16, 1863, she was a woman of great natural ability and good memory, and furnished many dates and other material for this genealogy.

ARCHIBALD M. ALLERTON.

(50)

48. VI. REUBEN[7], born at Cairo, July 25, 1788. He resided with his parents on the homestead farm; and after his father's death he carried on the business for his mother and sisters until his marriage, May 29, 1814, to Maria Miller, of Cairo. In the fall of the same year he served a short period with the militia during the war with Great Britain, but saw no actual hostilities. He then purchased a farm at Cairo, and cultivated it until 1825, when he became a minister of the Christian Church, and took charge of a church at Somerstown, in Westchester County. Afterwards he removed to South-East, in Putnam County, and continued to preach there until his death, January 28, 1832. He was possessed of little education but great natural ability, and was a man universally liked and esteemed.

49. VII. LUCY[7], born at Cairo, May 13, 1791. Married, March 15, 1815, Benjamin Bullock, of Greene Co. Died at Cairo, March 22, 1865.

DAVID[6] (23) had seven children.

50. I. ARCHIBALD MONTGOMERY[7], born at Canterbury, Connecticut, December, 3, 1780.

Removed with his parents to Dutchess County, New York, and there married, December 3, 1803, Rebecca Chamberlain. After his marriage he removed to Bloomingdale, New York City, and for many years conducted a drove yard or cattle market, known as the Upper Bull's Head. He was of an energetic disposition and a good talker, with an apparently inexhaustible fund of anecdotes. His first wife died October 20, 1832, and he married, September 28, 1833, Bathsheba Parks, and removed soon afterward to Broome County, where he became a farmer, and died at Upper Lisle, in that County, April 11, 1863. His second wife, by whom he had no children, died at the same place, August 29, 1863.

51. II. POLLY[7], born at Canterbury, February 14, 1783. Married in 1802 Philander Wilcox, of Madison County.

52. III. ISAAC[7], born at Canterbury, February 14, 1785. He accompanied his parents in childhood, first to Dutchess County, and afterward to Madison County. He decided at the age of 14 to become a Minister of the

Baptist Church, and it is said that before arriving at manhood he had charge of a congregation of Indian converts at Sangerfield. From 1805 to 1807 he preached at Hillsdale, New York, and in the latter year went to North-East, in Dutchess County. He was married, March 21, 1809, to Sylvia Winchell, daughter of Colonel Martin Winchell, of North-East. In the war of 1812, he acted as Chaplain in a militia regiment, and in 1815 assumed the charge of the Baptist Church at Sherburne, in Chenango County, New York, and in 1818, he went to Norwich, in the same County. From 1820 to 1840, he resided at New York City and in Putnam and Ulster Counties, and during this period he published several books on religious topics. From 1840 to 1849, he resided in the Town of Deer Park, in Orange County, and in the latter year he returned to Chenango County, and resided there and in the adjoining County of Broome, until his death, which occurred at Port Crane, in Broome County, February 14, 1875. He was thrice married, but had no children by his second and third wives.

53. IV. ANSON⁷, born at Amenia, May 14, 1787. Died at the age of 18, unmarried.
54. V. NANCY⁷, born at Amenia, October 10, 1790. Married, February 15, 1815, Calvin Owen, and after his death, married a Mr. Martin, of Greene County. Died in 1842.
55. VI. SALLY⁷, born at Amenia, October 15, 1792. Married, December 8, 1810, Isaac Dunham, of Tioga County, New York.
56. VII. JAMES⁷, born at Amenia, May 2, 1795. He was by occupation a mill-wright and machinist, and of a cheerful and reckless disposition. He married, in March, 1815, Jane Scott, and after her death he again married, August 14, 1830, Mrs. Harriet A. Dawson, a widow. Soon after his second marriage, in the fall of 1831, while at Baltimore making arrangements to move his family to that city, he disappeared and was supposed to have been drowned.

REUBEN⁶ (24) had seven children.
57. I. CORNELIUS⁷, born at Amenia, Dutchess County, New York, July 23, 1779. He received a good education and studied medicine and surgery under eminent prac-

titioners at New Haven, beginning practice at Pine Plains, in Dutchess County, in 1803. He married, September 22, 1813, Clarissa Heusted, and died at Pine Plains, April 26, 1855. He was successful as a physician, and esteemed by all for his charity and kindness of heart.

58. II. POLLY[7], born in 1781. Died in childhood.
59. III. LUCY[7], born at Amenia, in 1783. Married Thomas Barlow, and died at Amenia in 1860. She was famous as a beauty while young, and as a kind and worthy matron and mother in her later years.
60. IV. SAMUEL WATERS[7], born at Amenia, December 5, 1785. Married, March 26, 1808, Hannah Hurd. He resided at Amenia, about 57 years, and then moved to Yates County, New York, and became a farmer, and after residing there some 8 years he went west, but soon returned and settled in Wayne County, where he died at Newark, August 10, 1885, in his one hundredth year, having been for nearly a century an honest, upright man.
61. V. AMARYLLIS[7], born at Amenia, August 9, 1788. Died at Amenia, April 25, 1876, unmarried.

62. VI. Mira[7], born at Amenia, March 20, 1791. Married Taber Belden of Amenia, and died there in March, 1859.

63. VII. Milton Barlow[7], born at Amenia, August 21, 1799. Married, January 20, 1825, Eliza Belden. He was engaged all his life in mercantile business, first in a country store at Amenia, and afterwards in New York City, where he died suddenly, December 8, 1866.

Roger[6] (31) had four children.

64. I. Russell[7], born at Scituate, Rhode Island in 1789. He was a lawyer by occupation, and died November 16, 1815, unmarried.

65. II. Goodwin[7], born at Scituate, in 1792. He was a physician and surgeon, but died soon after beginning practice, May 12, 1819, unmarried.

66. III. John[7], born at Scituate in 1795. Died in 1830, unmarried.

67. IV. Jerusha[7], born at Scituate in 1797. Died unmarried, July 14, 1815.

The children of this family were all well educated and of more than average ability, but unfortunately inherited consumption from

THE ALLERTON FAMILY.   75

their mother, and all died of that disease in youth or early manhood.

JOHN⁶ (32) had four children.

68. I. JOHN RUSSELL⁷, born at Brooklyn, Connecticut, April 12, 1811. He married, September 25, 1842, the widow of his brother George, and died June 23, 1882. He was a farmer and a man of influence in local affairs, having filled various town offices and represented his native town, in which he resided all his life, in the Legislature. He furnished many details of his own branch of the family for this genealogy.

69. II. GEORGE⁷, born at Brooklyn, June 13, 1818. Married, March 13, 1839, Adaline Spaulding. Died April 6, 1842. He was a farmer by occupation.

70. III. WILLIAM⁷, born at Brooklyn, May 9, 1816. Died April 16, 1834, unmarried.

71. IV. MARY ANN⁷, born at Brooklyn, December 2, 1818. Died November 26, 1836, unmarried.

AMOS⁶ (36) had eight children.

72. I. ELIZABETH⁷, born about 1783.
73. II. JESSE⁷, born about 1785. Died at the age of eighteen.

74. III. Hannah[7], born about 1788. Died young and unmarried.

75. IV. David[7], born in Pennsylvania, in 1790. Married, December 15, 1812, Mary[7] (90). He moved to Stark County, Ohio, in 1816, and was a farmer and lumberman. He was killed by lightning, May 20, 1835.

76. V. Lavinia[7], born about 1793. She is said to have been twice married, first to a Mr. Patterson and second to a Mr. Nash.

77. VI. John[7], born in New Jersey, September 21, 1795. Married, February 11, 1817, Mary Husong. He was a farmer and resided nearly all his life at Euclid, Ohio. He died at Farmington, in that State, March 16, 1846.

78. VII. Amos[7], born near Munson, Miflin County, Pennsylvania, June 3, 1798.

He married Sophronia Laughlin, in 1821, but had no children. He was a farmer and of a roving disposition, but finally settled at Deerfield, Portage County Ohio, and died there June 3, 1879. He was a man of great ability, and in his later years was famous, locally, as a preacher in the Disciples Church.

79. VIII. A Daughter, who died in childhood.

MEAD ALLERTON.
(94)

JOHN⁶ (37) had eight children.

80. I. JACOB⁷, born in Crawford County, Pennsylvania, May 30, 1790. He was a lumberman by occupation, and died, unmarried, February 9, 1827.
81. II. POLLY⁷, born in Crawford County, Pennsylvania, about 1792. Married John Lupper, and died February 19, 1836.
82. III. JAMES⁷, born in Crawford County, Pennsylvania, August 16, 1796. Married, April 2, 1816, Mary Silvers. He resided in Stark County, Ohio, until 1848, when he moved to Huntington County, Indiana, where he died September 3, 1863. He was a farmer.
83. IV. RHODA⁷, born in Crawford County, Pennsylvania, May 30, 1800. She died young and unmarried.
84. V. PAMELA⁷, born at Crawford County, Pennsylvania, April 25, 1801. She married a tanner named Teel, and died September 20, 1838.
85. VI. RACHEL⁷, twin sister of Pamela. She married a farmer named Reeves, and died September 5, 1835.
86. VII. ABIGAIL⁷, born in Crawford County, Pennsylvania, July 19, 1803. She died young and unmarried.

87. VIII. JOHN[7], born in Crawford County, Pennsylvania, January 31, 1807. Married, June 9, 1828, Martha Hufman. He was a farmer and resided at Smithtown, Ohio, until 1875, when he moved to Alliance and resided there until his death, April 15, 1882.

STEPHEN[6] (38) had two children.

88. I. IRA[7], born at Shamokin, Northumberland County, Pennsylvania, September 22, 1797. He was never married.

89. II. JOHN LUTZ[7], born at Shamokin, Northumberland County Pennsylvania, November 5, 1799. Married, July 10, 1823, Hetta Mackey, of Coitsville, Ohio. He was a shoemaker, and resided nearly all his life at Coitsville, where he died, January 17, 1852.

JOB[6] (40) had four children.

90. I. MARY[7], born in New Jersey, in 1794. Married, December 15, 1812, her cousin David[7] (75). Died June 21, 1877.

91. II. JAMES[7], born in New Jersey, November 11, 1798. He married, in 1823 or 1824, Eleanor Kellogg, and resided at Deerfield, Portage County, Ohio, where he died in 1840.

92. III. SAMUEL[7], born near Baltimore, January 3, 1801. Married, in 1823, Elizabeth Pool, of Stark County, Ohio, who died December 27, 1823, after the birth of a son, John Porter Allerton[8]. In 1826, he married Mary Baughman, of Carroll County, Ohio. He was a blacksmith and farmer, a successful business man and a good citizen, and resided in Carroll and Stark Counties all his life. He died at Alliance, Ohio, January 11, 1870.

93. IV. THOMAS[7], born near Harper's Ferry, in 1804. Died young and unmarried.

THE EIGHTH GENERATION.

Joshua[7] (43) had nine children.

94. I. Mead[8], born at Cairo, Greene County, New York, February 2, 1805. He worked on his father's farm until manhood, attending school when the farm work allowed him to do so, and teaching himself in the winter of 1826. In 1827 and 1828 he conducted a country store at Gay Head, in Greene County; and from 1830 to 1844 he carried on the same business at Port Gibson, Ontario County, New York, where he was married, October 19, 1834, to Lavinia Blackmar, of Freehold, in Greene County. In 1860 he removed to Newark, in Wayne County, New York, where he resided until his death, February 19, 1884. He was an enterprising and successful business man, having acquired a competency and retired from active business before his removal to Newark, and was highly esteemed as a public spirited and influential

citizen wherever he resided. He was Supervisor of the Town of Manchester, in Ontario County, in 1846, 1847 and 1848. He had no children.

He was always deeply interested in the history of the old and honorable family, of which he was himself a worthy member, and after his retirement from business he devoted part of his time to the work of compiling a genealogy, and left a large and interesting manuscript, from which a great portion of the facts used in preparing the genealogical part of this work was obtained.

95. II. SARAH[8], born at Cairo, September 11, 1806. Married, September 11, 1832, James Cook. Died in Greene County, New York, February 14, 1873.

96. III. JOHN[8], born at Cairo, December 30, 1807. Committed suicide while insane from the effects of disease, May 25, 1851. Unmarried.

97. IV. LUCY ANN[8], born at Cairo, September 21, 1809. Died, unmarried, May 16, 1848.

98. V. RANSOM[8], born at Cairo, February 21, 1811. Married, March 2, 1847, Luvina R. Colson. He is a farmer and resides at Manchester,

Ontario County, New York. He is, since the death of Mead Allerton (94), the head of the Allerton family in the United States.

99.   VI. MARIAH[8], born at Cairo, August 12, 1813. Married, May 20, 1845, Cyrastus Betts, a farmer of Greene County, New York.

100. VII. WILLIAM C.[8], born at Cairo, June 11, 1815. Married, January 1, 1840, Esther Welsh, who died in 1841. Married again, February 22, 1843, Jane A. Green. He has been a farmer all his life at Gay Head, Greene County, New York, where he now resides.

101. VIII. JAMES[8], born at Cairo, March 29, 1817. Married, December 17, 1851, Eliza Ann Huntington. He was a farmer in Greene County, New York. Committed suicide while insane, at Greenville, in that county, February 4, 1869.

102. IX. ADALINE[8], born at Cairo, September 28, 1821. Married, May 20, 1845, Lewis Rundell, who died in 1859. Married again, October 28, 1869, Lemuel J. Swift.

ISAAC[7] (44) had eight children.

103. I. LUCY ANN[8], born in Greene County, New

THE ALLERTON FAMILY. 83

York, February 23, 1807. Married John Koon, a farmer and mechanic of Prattsburgh, Steuben County, New York.

104. II. ELIZA ANN[8], born in Greene County, February 14, 1808. Married Ebenezer L. Holcomb, of Ontario County, New York.

105. III. CAROLINE[8], born in Albany County, September 20, 1810. Married Ahira Chapin, a farmer, and removed to Wisconsin.

106. IV. TOWNSEND[8], born in Greene County, July 23, 1812. Married, February 1, 1838, Ann Chapin, and soon afterward removed to Savona, Steuben County, New York, where he now resides.

107. V. LEANDER[8], born in Greene County, June 1, 1814. Married, February 28, 1844, Jane Bryan, daughter of George Bryan. Removed to Steuben County, and was a lumberman and farmer, and a local politician of some note. He now resides at Savona, Steuben County, New York.

108. VI. DELANSON[8], born in Greene County, May 7, 1816. Married, February 10, 1848, Mary Jane Dudley. He is a farmer by occupation and now resides at Savona, Steuben County, New York.

109. VII. MARY JANE[8], born in Greene County, May 22, 1818. Married, November 17, 1841, Joshua Bryan, a farmer of Bath, New York.

110. VIII. JOHN T.[8], born at Benton, Yates County, New York, November 1, 1820. Married, November 10, 1848, Caroline Rapelyea. He was a farmer by occupation, and resided in Seneca County, New York, for eight years after his marriage. In 1856 he moved with his family to Kalamazoo County, Michigan, where he has ever since lived. He now resides in Galesburg, in that county, a prosperous and contented farmer.

JOHN[7] (45) had five children.

111. I. SALLY[8], born in Delaware County, New York, February 19, 1809. Married Barnabas A. Nichols, a farmer, of Monroe County, New York.

112. II. ANGELINA[8], born in Delaware County, March 16, 1811. Married Hiram G. Hemingway. Married again to Calvin Sweet, of Michigan.

113. III. CAROLINE[8], born in Delaware County, March 21, 1813. Died unmarried in 1834.

JOHN RUSSELL ALLERTON.
(68)

114. IV. ALMYRA[8], born in Delaware County, May 2, 1815. Married Peter M. Hess, and moved to Michigan.
115. V. JOHN[8], born in Delaware County, February, 1818. Died August, 1824.

REUBEN[7] (48) had seven children.

116. I. EMILY[8], born at Cairo, Greene County, New York, October 5, 1815. Married Levi Gage, a farmer, of Putnam County, New York.
117. II. GEORGE C.[8], born at Cairo, Greene County, December 2, 1817. Married, November 16, 1842, Hannah Hungerford. He was a machinist by occupation and resided nearly all his life at Elmira, Chemung County, New York, at which place he now lives.
118. III. EZRA[8], born at Cairo, Greene County, January 24, 1820. Married Marcia L. Hand. He was a farmer and resided in Greene County all his life. He died at Durham, in that County, September 23, 1859. He left no children.
119. IV. FRANCIS[8], born at Cairo, May 9, 1822. He went to California in 1849, and died there, unmarried, in 1851.

120.   V. Serena[8], born June 7, 1824. Died November 19, 1827.
121.   VI. Mary Ann[8], born in Putnam County, New York, March 11, 1827. Married, in 1860, John Norton, of Norton Hill, in Greene County, New York.
122.   VII. Emma E.[8], born in Putnam County, February 11, 1830. Is unmarried and resides at Poughkeepsie, New York.

Archibald Montgomery[7] (50) had nine children.

123.   I. Lucy Brigham[8], born November 20, 1804. Married Gervase Evans, a silversmith of New York City, and resides now at Mount Vernon, Westchester County, New York.
124.   II. George Washington[8], born December 25, 1806. Married, December 4, 1836, Margaret R. Dobbin, of New York City. Resided during the greater part of his life in New York City, where, like his father and brothers, he was engaged in the live-stock business. He was also a local politician of considerable note, and was several times elected Alderman. He died at Fordham, New York, August 14, 1870.

125. III. Anson Montgomery[8], born May 30, 1809. Married, December 18, 1838, Tamar H. Lockwood, and after her death, married again, May 21, 1851, Ann M. Austin. He was a farmer by occupation, and resided, until after his second marriage, in Dutchess County, New York; then moved to Illinois, and died in that State, June 9, 1863.

126. IV. William Chamberlain[8], born June 3, 1811. Died, unmarried, August 16, 1831.

127. V. Alice[8], born July 18, 1813. Died July 12, 1825.

128. VI. Jeannette Montgomery[8], born April 7, 1816. Married Rufus King Amory, of Binghamton, New York.

129. VII. David[8], born at Amenia, Dutchess County, New York, July 27, 1818. Married, January 25, 1845, Rachel Ward Hurd, daughter of Hebron Hurd, of Amenia. He was engaged in the live stock business in the City of New York all his life, with the exception of a trip to California in 1849 and 1850. For many years he was one of the owners of the stock-yards and cattle-markets at Fourth avenue and 44th street, and afterward at Third avenue

and 100th street. He was also largely interested in copper mining in the upper peninsula of Michigan; and during the war of the Rebellion he supplied the government with cattle and grain for the use of the army. He was an enterprising and successful business man and at one time was quite wealthy. He resided in New York City until 1864, when he removed to Mount Vernon, in Westchester County, where he died, March 3, 1877, and is buried in Woodlawn Cemetery.

130. VIII. ARCHIBALD MONTGOMERY[8], born February 14, 1821. Married, September 20, 1846, Charlotte A. Robson. He was connected in business with his brother David, during the lifetime of the latter, and accompanied him to California, and also removed from New York City to Mount Vernon, Westchester County, in 1864. He is now engaged in the coal business at New York.

131. IX. CHARLES HENRY[8], born August 6, 1824. Married, October —, 1855, Augusta Gorham. He was much of the time associated in business with his brothers, and like them he moved to Westchester County, and died

there at Tuckahoe, September 9, 1871. He had no children.

Isaac[7] (52) had eight children.

132. I. Clarissa[8], born at North-East, Dutchess County, New York, September 22, 1810. Died, unmarried, at New York City, March 7, 1829.

133. II. Sarah Ann[8], born at North-East, March 27, 1812. Married, February 15, 1832, Hamilton Eggleston. Died May 6, 1838. Had four children, three of whom died in infancy, and the fourth was killed at the battle of Gettysburg.

134. III. Horace W.[8], born at North-East, April 15, 1814. Married, December 10, 1835, Ann Eliza Otter. He has been a farmer and a dealer in live-stock. He resides at Port Jervis, New York.

135. IV. Mary Jane[8], born at Sherburne, Chenango County, New York, September 14, 1816. Married, April 5, 1835, Nicholas J. Eggleston, of North-East. Resides now at Chicago, Illinois.

136. V. Frances[8], born at Norwich, New York, July 17, 1818. Married Clark Durland,

of Deer Park, Orange County; and for her second husband, April 15, 1852, Jacob Ludwick, of Chenango County.

137. VI. JAMES M.[8], born on the schooner Neptune, off the coast of New Jersey, August 18, 1822. Married, April 4, 1848, Amelia S. Adams, who died July 14, 1860. He married again, November 14, 1861, Mary E. Goble, and for a third wife, June 3, 1885, Jennie E. Knight. He was a farmer in the town of Deer Park, in Orange County, New York, until 1869, when he was admitted to the Bar; his attention having been drawn to the legal profession by his successful defence of himself against a charge of assault and battery, which created great amusement at the time, and the report of which, first printed in a local paper, was widely copied. Since 1869, he has practiced law at Port Jervis, in Orange County, and although but poorly educated, his shrewdness and natural ability has made him quite successful.

138. VII. JOHN BELDING[8], born at Carmel, Putnam County, New York, in 1824. Died, unmarried, August 25, 1843.

139. VIII. Isaac[8], born in New York City, September 5, 1828. Married, April 4, 1852, Eliza McDaniel, daughter of Hiram McDaniel, of Chenango County, New York. He was a carpenter and joiner by occupation, and an inventor of several mechanical improvements. He resided in Deer Park, Orange County, and afterward at Port Crane, in Broome County, New York. From 1862 to 1865, he served in the Union Army during the war of the Rebellion, and in 1886, he moved to Killmaster, Alcona County, Michigan, where he now resides.

James[7] (56) had five children. The four oldest, all children of his first wife, died young, and left no descendants.

140. V. William Chamberlain[8], born at Greenburg, Westchester County, New York, November 8, 1831. Before his birth his father disappeared, as has been related. He was of a roving and unsettled disposition, but resided most of the time in Westchester County, New York, until 1874, when he moved to Van Buren County, Michigan, where he was a farmer, and also worked at his trade of

carpenter and joiner. Married, March 7, 1852, Elizabeth Lafarge. He now resides at Kendall, Van Buren County, Michigan.

CORNELIUS[7] (57) had four children.

141. I. REUBEN[8], born at Pine Plains, Dutchess County, New York, September 2, 1814. Died April 16, 1816.
142. II. AN INFANT, died in infancy, unnamed.
143. III. MARY[8], born at Pine Plains, February 15, 1817. Married, May 6, 1850, Fitzalan Stebbins, of Penn Yan, New York. Died in 1853.
144. IV. CORNELIUS[8], born at Pine Plains, May 19, 1819. He was physician and surgeon, and a man of fine natural abilities, but erratic and indolent. He died suddenly at Dover Plains, Dutchess County, January 15, 1867. He was never married.
145. V. SARAH H.[8], born at Pine Plains, July 27, 1826. She was a teacher by occupation. Died at Pine Plains, in April, 1859, unmarried.

SAMUEL W.[7] (60) had nine children.

146. I. CORNELIA[8], born at Amenia, Dutchess County, New York, March 26, 1809. Married Walter Sherman, a farmer of Amenia.

147. II. AMARYLLIS[8], born at Amenia, January 1, 1812. Married Shadrac Sherman, of New York City.

148. III. HENRY R.[8], born at Amenia, December 25, 1814. He went to Illinois in early manhood, but soon returned to Wayne County, New York, residing first at Arcadia, and afterward at Newark, where he now lives. He was never married.

149. IV. ORVILLE HURD[8], born at Amenia, April 17, 1817. Married, January 15, 1845, Eliza Adelaide Dean, of Dresden, Yates County, New York. At thirteen he began life as a clerk in a country store, and in 1843, in partnership with Walter Sherman and William Taber he opened a store at Newark, Wayne County, New York, and continued in that business until 1868, when he moved to Pittsburg, Pennsylvania, and for seventeen years was Superintendent of the Pennsylvania Central Stock Yards at that place. In 1885, he resigned that position and returned to Newark, where he now resides in the well earned enjoyment of a comfortable fortune.

150. V. AMANDA H.[8], born at Amenia, July 15,

1818. Married William Taber, who was afterward engaged in business with her brother, Orville H.

151. VI. Byron[8], born at Amenia, September 20, 1822. Married, September 22, 1868, Helen Sherman, of Dover Plains, Dutchess County, New York. He is a farmer, and resides at Newark, Wayne County, New York.

152. VII. Rebecca H.[8], born at Amenia, September 28, 1824. She resides at Newark, New York, and is unmarried,

153. VIII. Lois J.[8], born at Amenia, January 26, 1826. She resides at Newark, New York, and is unmarried.

154. IX. Samuel Waters[8], born at Amenia, May 26, 1828. Married, July 1, 1860, Pamilla W. Thompson, of Peoria, Illinois, and after her death, married again, March 15, 1882, Agnes C. Thompson, a sister of his first wife. He began business as a dealer in live-stock at Newark, New York, but soon went to Illinois, and finally settled in Chicago, where he now resides. In addition to his business as a dealer in live-stock, and a shipper of stock and dressed meats, he has been largely interested in other enterprises,

having been one of the founders of the First National Bank of Chicago, and taking a leading part in the introduction of the Cable Railway in that City. He is an energetic and enterprising man of business, and is very wealthy, and highly respected throughout the section of the country, to the development of whose natural resources he has devoted his attention.

MILTON B.[7] (63) had six children.

155. I. CLARA[8], born at Washington, Dutchess County, New York, December 30, 1825. Died, unmarried, November 21, 1874.
156. II. MARY E.[8], born at Washington, December 7, 1827. Died, unmarried, November 19, 1875.
157. III. ELIPHA B.[8], born at Amenia, December 7, 1829. Married, June 21, 1853, George H. Petrie. Died, November 29. 1853.
158. IV. GEORGE MILTON[8], born at Washington, Dutchess County, New York, December 1, 1831. Married, October 5, 1858, Lois Mabbett, of Dover, New York. Married again, January 24, 1877, Mary Alida Leggett. He was engaged in the manufacture

of rubber goods all his life, being for many years connected with the Goodyear India Rubber Glove Manufacturing Company, of New York City and Naugatuck, Connecticut. He resided at New York City until 1867, when he removed to Naugatuck, and resided there until his death, December 2, 1882. He was a man of great ability and of the highest character, active in business and society, generous, hospitable and public spirited.

159. V. REUBEN GERMAN[8], born at Dover Plains, Dutchess County, New York, October 20, 1834. Married, September 19, 1866, Henrietta L. Vredenburgh, daughter of Robert M. Vredenburgh, of New York City. He resided at New York City and was engaged in the rubber business with his brother. He was a famous angler, one of the founders of "The Oquossoc Club," of the Rangely Lakes, in Maine, and author of a work on angling. He died at the City of New York, June 18, 1877.

160. VI. ANNIE E.[8], born at Dover Plains, October 20, 1836. She is unmarried and resides at New York City.

THE ALLERTON FAMILY. 97

JOHN RUSSELL[7] (68) had six children.

161. I. FRANCES ADELINE[8], born at Brooklyn, Connecticut, August 6, 1843. Married, in 1870, Daniel W. Purinton, of Worcester, Mass.

162. II. ABBY[8], born at Brooklyn, October 12, 1845. Died, unmarried, September 6, 1860.

163. III. JANE[8], twin sister of Abby[8], born at Brooklyn, October 12, 1845. Died, unmarried, January 7, 1866.

164. IV. HENRY[8], born at Brooklyn, January 29, 1848. Married, October 10, 1870, Maria Neff. And after her death married again, September 6, 1885, Mrs. Abby M. Porter. He resided on the farm at Brooklyn until 1876, and he is now a resident of Lawrence, Massachusetts, where he is connected with the local telegraph and telephone company.

165. V. JOHN[8], born January 1, 1854, Died July 5, 1854.

166. VI. CHARLES[8], born June 15, 1855. Died December 9, 1862.

GEORGE[7] (69) had one child.

167. I. MARY ANN[8], born February 4th, 1840. Died July 14, 1841.

DAVID[7] (75) had thirteen children.

168. I. SAMUEL[8], born in Chester County, Pennsylvania, June 8, 1814. Married, October 5, 1837, Amelia Swope. He resided at Mapleton, Stark County Ohio, and was engaged in business as an auctioneer, and filled many local offices. He died at Mapleton, March 4, 1887.

169. II. JOHN[8], born in Stark County, Ohio, July 31, 1815. Died August 24, 1815.

170. III. JOB[8], born in Stark County, Ohio, July 27, 1816. Died September 3, 1838.

171. IV. AMOS[8], born in Stark County, Ohio, February 14, 1818. Died May 1, 1826.

172. V. MARIA[8], born in Stark County, Ohio. November 4, 1819. Married in August, 1845, William McDonnel.

173. VI. HANNAH[8], born in Stark County, Ohio, May 15, 1821. Married, in 1843, Joseph Headley.

174. VII. ELEANOR[8], born in Stark County, Ohio, October 10, 1824. Died August 23, 1828.

175. VIII. IRA[8], born in Stark County, Ohio, June 28, 1827. Died March 27, 1829.

176. IX. MARY ANNE[8], born in Stark County, Ohio, March 30, 1829. Married John

Pemble, and now resides at Bement, Piatt County, Illinois.

177. X. ROSANNA[8], born in Stark County, Ohio, November 3, 1830. Married, in April, 1848, Timothy Sheares.

178. XI. DAVID[8], born Stark County, Ohio, March 31. 1833. Died, unmarried, in 1846.

179. XII. DANIEL[8], twin brother of David. Died January 4, 1834.

180. XIII. JAMES[8], born in Stark County, Ohio, August 20, 1835. Married, January 3, 1857, Elizabeth Vanostan, of Stark County, who died, December 19, 1866. Married again, December 3, 1868, Mary A. Niewander, also of Stark County. He is a farmer, and resided in Pike township, Stark County, Ohio, until 1871, when he moved to Barry County, Michigan, and settled at Nashville, where he now resides.

JOHN[7] (77) had eleven children.

181 I. ELIZABETH[8], born at Euclid, Ohio, May 1, 1819. Married Dwight Selden, of Cleveland, Ohio.

182. II. AMOS[8], born at Euclid, April 3, 1821. Died, unmarried, July 28, 1840.

183. III. Chloe[8], born at Euclid, May 17, 1823. Married Charles Tilden, of Jefferson County, Wisconsin.

184. IV. Dorcas[8], born May 27, 1825. Married Addison House, of Cleveland, Ohio. Married second time, Moses Warren, of the same place.

185. V. Isaac Chauncey[8], born at Euclid, April 10, 1827. Married in 1853, Fannie Glines. Married again in 1865, Elvira A. Giddings. He died, July 5, 1885, leaving one child, a daughter.

186. VI. Oliver Hazard Perry[8], born at Euclid, March 30, 1829. Married, December 26, 1852, Harriet Robertson. He moved to Wisconsin when sixteen years old, and soon after became a carpenter and joiner. Returning to Ohio in 1850, he worked there at his trade a few years, when he again went to Wisconsin, and opened a store at Dayton, at the same time doing business as a builder and contractor. In 1857, he gave up his store, and from then until 1883, he resided successively at Leroy, Aztalon and Eureka, carrying on a farm at each place, and continuing his business as a builder. In 1883, he again opened a store

ORVILLE H. ALLERTON.

at Berlin, and in 1887, he moved to Antigo, Langlade County, where he now resides, engaged in the same business.

187. VII. ALPHEUS BURTON[8], born at Euclid, Ohio, February 18, 1831. Married for his first wife, October 16, 1852, Amanda Hoyt; for his second wife, September 8, 1862, Ellen P. Palmer, of Allegany, well known as a writer of poems of some merit. He was by occupation a farmer and builder, and lived from boyhood up to 1879, at Lake Mills, Jefferson County, Wisconsin, and in that year moved to Hamlin, Brown County, Kansas, where he now resides.

188. VIII. MARY[8], born at Euclid, Ohio, March 5, 1833. Married for her first husband, Seneca Fuller; and for her second husband, Perry Hyer. Resides at Aztalon, Marathon County, Wisconsin.

189. IX. SARAH JANE[8], born February 24, 1835. Died, May 23, 1836.

190. X. GEORGE W.[8], born at Euclid, February 19, 1831. Died, April 3, 1837.

191. XI. SYBIL FRANCES[8], born at Euclid, March 14, 1839. Married Luke Leatherdale, and resides at Spencer, Marathon County, Wisconsin.

James[7] (82) had eleven children.

192. I. Rachel[8], born in Stark County, Ohio, January 31, 1817. Married, March 30, 1843, John Weaver.

193. II. Sarah[8], born in Stark County, Ohio, December 6, 1818. Married, November 10, 1842, Samuel Fulmer, and died January 12, 1861.

194. III. Asa[8], born in Stark County, Ohio, January 16, 1821. He went to California in 1849, and is supposed to have died there, unmarried.

195. IV. Amos[8], born in Stark County, Ohio, March 7, 1823. Married, about 1849, Rebecca Baum. He was a farmer in Huntington County, Indiana. Died, October 12, 1872.

196. V. Sophronia[8], born in Stark County, Ohio, December 27, 1825. Married, December 20, 1849, Levi Denius.

197. VI. John[8], born in Stark County, Ohio, April 9, 1828. Married, September 11, 1853, Nancy Peigh. He was a farmer in Stark County, until the outbreak of the Rebellion, when he joined the Union Army and died of disease contracted while in service, at Evansville, Indiana, May 2, 1862.

198. VII. James[8], born in Stark County, Ohio, July 22, 1830. He was a farmer, and died unmarried, in Huntington County, Indiana, March 14, 1858.

199. VIII. David S.[8], born in Stark County, Ohio, August 15, 1832. Died, unmarried, in Huntington County, Indiana, October 12, 1853.

200. IX. Hester[8], born in Stark County, Ohio, February 20, 1835. Married Samuel Fulmer, of Gar Creek, Allen County, Indiana.

201. X. Mary[8], born in Stark County, Ohio, December 29, 1836. Married Emanuel Kinnel, of Fostoria, Seneca County, Ohio.

202. XI. Ezekiel[8], born in Stark County, Ohio, April 22, 1839. Married, January 1, 1865, Margaret Gibson. When nine years old he went with his parents to Huntington County, Indiana, then a wilderness, and has resided there ever since. He now lives at Roanoke, in that county, and is a farmer by occupation.

John[7] (87) had ten children.

203. I. Hiram[8], born at Smithtown, Mahoning County, Ohio, May 18, 1830. Married,

September 17, 1854, Lois Bailer, daughter of Peter Bailer, of Mahoning County, Ohio. He resides at Hartford, Van Buren County, Michigan.

204. II. Andrew J.[8], born at Smithtown, May 21, 1831. Married, October 22, 1857, Martha Babcock, daughter of Isaac Babcock, of Providence, Wood County, Ohio. He is a farmer and resides at Keelersville, Van Buren County, Michigan.

205. III. Esther A.[8], born at Smithtown, May 14, 1833. Died, unmarried, September 24, 1876.

206. IV. Mary K.[8], born at Smithtown, September 26, 1835. Married, December 25, 1866, Joshua Barnaby, of Alliance. She resides now near Benton Harbor, Michigan.

207. V. Alvira[8], born at Smithtown, November 26, 1837. Married E. N. Hartshorn, of Mount Union, Stark County, Ohio.

208. VI. William H.[8], born at Smithtown, February 10, 1841. Married, October 30, 1868, Amelia Scranton, of Lexington, Stark County, Ohio. He served in the Union Army and was taken prisoner at the battle of Stone River, and confined for a

time in Libby Prison. He is now a manufacturer of brick at Alliance, Ohio.

209.   VII. ALMOND[8], born at Smithtown, November 16, 1843. He served in the Union Army and was killed at the battle of Stone River, December 31, 1862.

210.   VIII. JOHN[8], born at Smithtown, September 20, 1845. Married, April 18, 1877, Fannie E. Hanson. He resided at Smithtown until 1870, when he moved to Hartford, Van Buren County, Michigan, where he now lives. He is a manufacturer of pumps, and also a mover of buildings.

211.   IX. FRANCIS[8], born at Smithtown, February 28, 1848. Married, October 24, 1872, Henrietta Oby, daughter of Joseph Oby, of Alliance, Ohio. He is a farmer, and resides at Keelersville, Van Buren County, Michigan.

212.   X. FRIEND J.[8], born at Smithtown, December, 21, 1850. Died April 25, 1853.

JOHN L.[7] (89) had eleven children.

213.   I. STEPHEN WHITMORE[8], born at Coitsville, Mahoning County, Ohio, June 11, 1824. Died, unmarried, in 1862, at Louisville, Kentucky, while serving in the Union Army.

214. II. ADMETUS OGDEN[8], born at Coitsville, October 30, 1825. He served through the Mexican war, and soon after returning home, died, September 28, 1848. He was never married.

215. III. MARY L.[8], born at Coitsville, May 16, 1827. Married William Alander, a farmer, of Espyville, Pennsylvania.

216. IV. ABIGAIL M.[8], born at Coitsville, April 1, 1829. Married Thomas Hogg, a farmer, of Coitsville, and now resides at Hollis, Kansas.

217. V. CATHERINE L.[8], born at Coitsville, July 7, 1830. Married Henry F. Holden, of Michigan. Died in 1860.

218. VI. TERESSA B.[8], born at Coitsville, February 15, 1833. Married Harvey Hill, a farmer, of Lyme, Ohio.

219. VII. ESTER O,[8], born at Coitsville, November 16, 1834. Married George B. St. John, a merchant, of Toledo, Ohio.

220. VIII. IRA[8], born at Coitsville, December 15, 1837. Married, November 28, 1866, Mary A. Hoagg, daughter of Samuel G. Hoagg, of Canandaigua, New York. He is a farmer, and resides at Roxana, Eaton County, Michigan.

221. IX. HANNAH R.[8], born at Coitsville, March 6, 1840. Married Addison Randall, a farmer, of East Hubbard, Ohio.

222. X. LEMIRA C.[8], born at Coitsville, August 22, 1842. Is unmarried and resides at Youngstown, Ohio. Some valuable information for this work was obtained from her.

223. IX. JOHN[8], born at Coitsville, August 17, 1844. Married, November 9, 1868, Amanda Campbell, of Kalamo, Michigan. He was of a roving disposition, and while in a lumber camp in Northern Michigan, in the winter of 1881-82, he was accidentally killed.

JAMES[7] (91) had five children.

224. I. OLIVER H.[8], born at Deerfield, Portage County, Ohio, May 25, 1825. Married, August 20, 1848, Sarah McCoy. He resided for a time at Angola, Steuben County, Indiana, and at East Fairfield, Columbiana County, Ohio, but was of a roving disposition, and eventually went to California, where he is supposed to have died.

225. II. CATHERINE[8], born at Deerfield, April 8, 1827. Died April 9, 1846.

226. III. SARAH[8], born at Deerfield, November 9, 1829. Married, August 21, 1851, Stephen Randall. She died July 29, 1869.
227. IV. ELEANOR[8], born at Deerfield, March 19, 1833. Died August 25, 1835.
228. V. JAMES[8], born at Deerfield, January 2, 1836. Died April 14, 1837.

SAMUEL[7] (92) had twelve children.

229. I. JOHN PORTER[8], born at Waynesburgh, Ohio, December 16, 1823. Married, in April, 1849, Sarah T. Sargent, of New Albany, Indiana, and soon after settled at Louisville, Kentucky, where he still resides. He is a moulder by trade, and a man of unusually fine appearance. He has no children.
230. II. SAMUEL[8], born at Waynesburgh, September 9, 1827. Married, August 12, 1852, Jane G. Mitchner. Was engaged in many kinds of business, principally in connection with the coal and iron trade, and resided nearly all his life at Salem, Ohio. Died at Salem, December 9, 1879.
231. III. ZACHARIAH[8], born at Waynesburgh, Ohio, April 14, 1829. Married, in April, 1852, Sarah Hartzell. Married again, January 9,

SAMUEL W. ALLERTON.
(154)

1881, Eva Partello. He served in the Union Army, during the Rebellion, and is now in the National Soldiers' Home, at Dayton, Ohio.

232. IV. GEORGE W.[8], born at Waynesburgh, Ohio, November 16, 1830. He was a saddler and harness maker, at Terre Haute, Indiana, and was very successful in business. He was never married, and was killed while on a hunting expedition about 1868.

233. V. WILLIAM[8], born at Waynesburgh, Ohio, December 13, 1832. Married, December 31, 1854, Elizabeth McKee. He is a painter, and machinist, and resides at New Castle, Lawrence County, Pennsylvania.

234. VI. ENOCH[8], born at Waynesburgh, Ohio, June 16, 1835. Married, in 1856, Mary Knapp. Died at Cincinnatti, December 16, 1866.

235. VII. MARY ELIZABETH[8], born January 24, 1837. Married, July 2, 1857, John Joseph. Died February 21, 1877.

236. VIII. ISABELLA[8], born November 25, 1839. Married, July 2, 1857, James Kynett, of Canton, Ohio. Resides now at Alliance.

237. IX. JACOB[8], born at Waynesburg, Ohio, May 4, 1841. He served in the Union Army,

during the war of the Rebellion, and lost one eye in battle. He was never married, and now resides at Washington, D. C.

238. X. RACHAEL E.[8], born September 22, 1844. She was never married; resides now at Adriance, Michigan.

239. XI. CALISTA[8], born August 25, 1847. Married, Richard W. Teeters, of Alliance, where she now resides.

240. XII. ISAAC[8], born in Carroll County, Ohio, November 23, 1850. Married, September 27, 1877, Susan McLaughlin. He is a carpenter and builder, and resides at Dell Roy, Carroll County, Ohio.

THE NINTH GENERATION.

Ransom⁸ (98) has eight children.

241. I. Florence⁹, born at Manchester, Ontario County, New York, November 20, 1848. Married, October 16, 1872, Seneca Short, a farmer of Port Gibson, New York.

242. II. Frederick Mead⁹, born at Manchester, December 26, 1850. Married, October 23, 1878, Cornelia Sherman, of Arcadia, Wayne County. Married again, November 25, 1885, Minnie A. Rogers. He resides at Newark, Wayne County, New York, and is engaged in the produce business. He has no children.

243. III. Theron Yeomans⁹, born at Manchester, March 5, 1853. Married, February 3, 1886, Ann Huldah Chapman. He now resides at Manchester, and has no children.

244. IV. Mary⁹, born at Manchester, February 15, 1855. She resides at Rochester, New York, and is at present unmarried.

245. V. Anna⁹, born at Manchester, December 25,

1856. She resides at Rochester, New York, and is unmarried.

246. VI. Lucy[9], born at Manchester, November 27, 1859. She is unmarried. and resides with her parents at Manchester.

247. VII. Augusta[9], born at Manchester, May 27, 1863. She is unmarried, and resides with her parents.

248. VIII. Edith[9], born at Manchester, June 10, 1867. She is unmarried, and resides with her parents at Manchester.

William C.[8] (100) has nine children.

249. I. Ransom Welch[9], born at Greenville, Greene County, New York, December 2, 1840. Married, February 3, 1863, Letitia Betts. He is a farmer, and now resides at Gay Head, Greene County, New York.

250. II. Leonard Green[9], born in Greene County, June 11, 1845. Married, January 9, 1867, Mary Stevens. He is a farmer, and resides at Gay Head, Greene County, New York. During the war of the Rebellion, he served in the Union Army, from the beginning of the struggle to its close, having enlisted when only nineteen.

251. III. REUBEN GERMAN[9], born in Greene County, December 14, 1846. He died September 23, 1872, unmarried.
252. IV. CAROLINE ELIZABETH[9], born August 9, 1849. Is unmarried and resides with her father.
253. V. HARRIET[9], born in 1852. Died in infancy.
254. VI. LODEMA[9], born in 1853. Died in infancy.
255. VII. ADALINE J.[9], born January 30, 1854. Is unmarried, and resides with her father at Gay Head, Greene County, New York.
256. VIII. WILLIAM MYRON[9], born at Cairo, Greene County, December 27, 1855. Married, December 13, 1882, Hannah Hoge. He is a farmer, and resides at Sheridan, Sheridan County, Kansas.
257. IX. JAMES MEAD[9], born at Greenville, July 11, 1861. He is a farmer, and resides with his father at Gay Head, Greene County, New York, and is unmarried.

JAMES[8] (101) had two children.
258. I. WALTER MEAD[9], born at Cairo, Greene County, New York, May 29, 1853. Died, at Cincinnati, Ohio, in 1874, unmarried.
259. II. MARY CATHARINE[9], born at Cairo, May 9, 1857.

Townsend[8] (106) has six children.

260.   I. Judson[9], born in Steuben County, New York, November 25, 1838. He served in the Union Army during the war of the Rebellion, and afterwards went west. He now resides at Emmettsville, Ada County, Idaho, and is unmarried.

261.   II. Lamar[9], born April 11, 1841. Died August 28, 1845.

262.   III. Luthera[9], born in Steuben County, March 28, 1843. She is unmarried, and resides at Savona, Steuben County, New York.

263.   IV. Annette[9], born in Steuben County, January 15, 1846. Married, November 19, 1865, Isaac Nobles, a farmer, of Savona, Steuben County, New York.

264.   V. Emily[9], born in Steuben County, February 9, 1849. Married, May 11, 1871, George Beaton, and after his death, married again, January 14, 1880, James Milford Andrews, of Syracuse.

265.   VI. Frank C.[9], born in Steuben County, January 13, 1855. Married, May 13, 1877, Emma Collson, of Thurston, Steuben County, New York. He is a farmer, and resides at Thurston.

LEANDER[8] (107) has four children.

266. I. SOPHIA[9], born in Steuben County, New York, August 14, 1846. Married, August 7, 1873, Edmund P. Hewlett, a farmer, of San Rafael, California.

267. II. GEORGE[9], born in Steuben County, August 4, 1848. He is unmarried, and in the employ of the Wisconsin Central Railroad Company, at Saginaw City, Michigan.

268. III. ELIZABETH[9], born in Steuben County, May 5, 1851. She is unmarried, and resides with her father, at Savona, Steuben County, New York.

269. IV. CHARLES BRADFORD[9], born in Steuben County, April 28, 1856. He is unmarried, a farmer by occupation, and resides with his father, at Savona, New York.

DELANSON[8] (108) has four children.

270. I. FRANCES CAROLINE[9], born in Steuben County, New York, February 26, 1849. Married, September 27, 1876, Adam Parker, of San Francisco.

271. II. SARAH[9], born in Steuben County, April 26, 1854. Is unmarried.

272. III. DUDLEY[9], born in Steuben County, May

20, 1859. He is a farmer at Savona, Steuben County, New York. Is unmarried.

273. IV. MARY[9], born in April, 1866. Died in infancy.

JOHN T.[8] (110) has six children.

274. I. HURON[9], born at Bath, Steuben County, New York, November 14, 1848. Married, November 25, 1883, Eliza Guthrie, of Mancelona, Michigan. He is a farmer and speculator, and in prosperous circumstances, and resides at Mancelona.

275. II. KATE CHARLOTTE[9], born April 2, 1851. Died, unmarried, March 21, 1864.

276. III. IDA[9], born at Covert, Seneca County, New York, November 25, 1853. Married, January 8, 1878, Aaron H. Carr, of Galesburgh, Michigan.

277. IV. FREDERICK WOODWORTH[9], born at Covert, Seneca County, New York, April 9, 1856. Married, June 9, 1885, Jennie Guthrie, of Elk Rapids, Michigan. He is associated with his brother Huron in business, and resides at Mancelona, Michigan.

278. V. MARY ELLEN[9], born at Comstock, Kalamazoo County, Michigan, March 19, 1859. Married,

GEORGE W. ALLERTON.
(12())

February 22, 1887, Addison J. Plank, of Anoka, Minnesota.

279. VI. LIZZIE CAROLINE[9], born at Comstock, Kalamazoo County, Michigan, September 28, 1867.

GEORGE C.[8] (117) has two children.

280. I. WILLIS R.[9], born June 14, 1846. Died June 9, 1848.
281. II. FRANK H.[9], born at Westerlo, Albany County, New York, September 21, 1849. Married, August 21, 1873, Alice T. Hoffman, of Elmira, New York. Resided until 1885, at Elmira, where he was employed as a salesman. He now keeps a general store at Painted Post, Steuben County, New York.

GEORGE W.[8] (124) had ten children.

282. I. ALICE REBECCA[9], born November 29, 1836. Died March 15, 1837.
283. II. CHARLOTTE BAILEY[9], born at New York City, December 23, 1837. Married, March 11, 1858, William C. Burmiston, of New York.
284. III. JAMES DOBBIN[9], born at New York City, January 10, 1839. Killed by the accidental

discharge of a gun, while hunting, April 14, 1860.

285. IV. JOSEPHINE[9], born at New York City, February 28, 1841. Married, June 8, 1865, John D. Young, of New York City.

286. V. GEORGE WASHINGTON[9], born at New York City, March 17, 1843. Married, February 1, 1866, Elizabeth R. Judd, daughter of William Judd, of Kent, Connecticut. He is now the proprietor of a cattle ranch at Albright, Custer County, Montana.

287. VI. MARY GREENWOOD[9], born at New York City, November 29, 1846. Married, November 29, 1865, William Merritt, of New York City. Died January 23, 1875.

288. VII. MARGARET LOUISA[9], born at New York City, February 17, 1848. Married, August 19, 1869, Isaac D. Darke, of New York City. Died November 1, 1875.

289. VIII. ELIZA MILLER[9], born at New York City, March 24, 1850. She is unmarried, and resides at Rye, New York.

290. IX. DAVID DYCKMAN[9], born at New York City, May 29, 1853. Married, July 28, 1886, Mary Emma Matthews, daughter of William S. Matthews, of Jersey City. He is now

in the grain elevating business, and resides in Jersey City, New Jersey.

291. X. CHARLES HENRY[9], born May 9, 1856. Died January 19, 1858.

ANSON MONTGOMERY[8] (125) had eight children.

292. I. ALMYRA PARDEE[9], born April 20, 1840. Married, March 28, 1860, Hamilton Bingham.
293. II. ALICE REBECCA[9], born March 7, 1843. Married, May 17, 1865, Ellery Stebbins, of Clinton, New York.
294. III. ABBY LOCKWOOD[9], born April 24, 1846. Married, January 14, 1866, John A. Edwards.
295. IV. LEWIS PURDY[9], born April 7, 1847. Died in infancy.
296. V. CHARLES HENRY[9], born May 6, 1852. He is a civil engineer, and resides at Bellingham, Whatcom County, Washington Territory.
297. VI. WILLIAM CHAMBERLAIN[9], born December 31, 1854. He is a hat manufacturer, and resides at Danbury, Connecticut.
298. VII. MINNIE[9], born October 29, 1862. Married, October 24, 1881, Samuel B. Mead, who died October 29, 1882; and for her second

husband, September 9, 1886, Edward P. Allen, of New York City.

299. VIII. ARCHIBALD MONTGOMERY[9], born January 4, 1864. He resides with the widow of his uncle Charles[8] (131), at Tuckahoe, Westchester County, New York, and is unmarried.

DAVID[8] (129) had nine children.

300. I. ELIZA JEANNETTE[9], born at the City of New York, November 19, 1845. Married, February 19, 1876, Rev. William Berrian Hooper, an Episcopalian clergyman, and resides now (January, 1888), at Portchester, Westchester County, New York.

301. II. AMY BARLOW[9], born at Amenia, Dutchess County, New York, July 29, 1847. Married, April 12, 1870, William Augustus Hustace, and resides at Mount Vernon, Westchester County, New York.

302. III. DAVID[9], born at the City of New York, July 3, 1851. Married, September 25, 1879, Matilda Christine Salisbury, daughter of Thomas Salisbury, of London, England. He is a fruit farmer and resides at Marlborough, Ulster County, New York.

303. IV. WALTER SCOTT[9], born at the City of New York, October 4, 1852. Married, January 24, 1884, Adelaide Hersom, daughter of Andrew J. Hersom, of Berwick, York County, Maine. He graduated from Columbia College in 1874, was in the employ of the Chicago and Northwestern Railway Company at Chicago in 1875, returned to New York in the winter of that year and began the study of law, and was admitted to the bar in 1877, at Poughkeepsie, New York. Is now a practicing lawyer in New York City, and resides at Mount Vernon, Westchester County, New York. He has always taken a great interest in the history of the Allerton family, and is the author of this work.

304. V. RUFUS KING[9], born at the City of New York, October 1, 1854. Married, June 17, 1882, Lavinia Irish, daughter of Samuel Knight Irish, of Warboys, Huntingdonshire, England. He was for several years a stock and mining broker in New York City, and made several trips to England, where he was married. Is now a farmer and resides at Whitneys Point, Broome County, New York.

305. VI. WILLIAM BEAL[9], born at New York City, February 15, 1857. Died February 5, 1860.
306. VII. RACHEL BERRY[9], born at New York City, June 15, 1859, Married, January 25, 1883, John B. Berry, a civil engineer in the employ of the Chicago and Northwestern Railway Company, and resides at Chicago.
307. VIII. MARY SIBLEY[9], born at New York City, January 31, 1863. Is at present unmarried, and resides with her mother at Binghamton, New York.
308. IX. FREDERICK SIBLEY[9], born at Mount Vernon, Westchester County, New York, May 16, 1866. Died March 10, 1870.

ARCHIBALD MONTGOMERY[8] (130) has three children.

309. I. MARY LOUISA[9], born at New York City, July 15, 1847. Died May 15, 1850.
310. II. GEORGE ROBSON[9], born at New York City, April 10, 1851. Married, September 30, 1885, Marian Hungerford.
311. III. CHARLOTTE A.[9], born at New York City, June 22, 1855. Married, January 3, 1883, Ernest Staples.

Horace W.[8] (134) has seven children.

312. I. George W.[9], born at Deer Park, Orange County, New York, July 10, 1838. Died in infancy.
313. II. Sylvia Ann[9], born at New Paltz, Ulster County, New York, November 28, 1836. Married, October 7, 1857, Gustavus Bramm.
314. III. Eleanor L.[9], born at Deer Park, July 17, 1842. Married, December 23, 1862, Charles Williams.
315. IV. Matilda[9], born at Deer Park, August 30, 1848. Married, June 23, 1875, George E. Truex.
316. V. Sarah C.[9], born at Deer Park, February 11, 1852. Married, January 1, 1872, Moses Smith, of Deposit, New York.
317. VI. Mary E.[9], born at Deer Park, February 1, 1856. She is a nurse by occupation and unmarried.
318. VII. William H.[9], born at Deer Park, October 17, 1858. Married, September 24, 1884, Antoinette Stidd. He is a photographer and resides at Port Jervis.

James M.[8] (137) has eleven children.
319. I. Mary Maria[9], born at Deer Park, Orange

County, New York, January 11, 1849. Married, October 27, 1870, Joseph Wilkin.

320. II. ALEXANDER W.[9], born at Deer Park, August 27, 1850. Died May 22, 1857.

321. III. GERTRUDE A.[9], born at Deer Park, February 22, 1852. Married, October 2, 1873, Howell P. Stone.

322. IV. CHAUNCEY JAMES[9], born at Deer Park, January 3, 1854. Died December 22, 1856.

323. V. SUSAN LOUISE[9], born at Deer Park, April 28, 1856. Married, December 28, 1875, George Baker.

324. VI. GEORGE OLIVER[9], born at Deer Park, May 30, 1858. Married, February 22, 1880, Sarah Harding. He is a railroad employee, and resides at Port Jervis, New York.

325. VII. AMBROSE B.[9], born at Port Jervis, New York, November 10, 1862. Died in infancy.

326. VIII. ADELLA M.[9], born at Port Jervis, December 18, 1865. Married, October 7, 1883, Frank Burns.

327. IX. IRA.[9], born at Port Jervis, February 10, 1868. Died, at Fort Worth, Texas, December 12, 1887, unmarried.

328. X. MAURICE[9], born at Port Jervis, February 25, 1870. Died December 13, 1879.

ORVILLE H. ALLERTON.
C '48

THE ALLERTON FAMILY. 125

329. XI. Norman[9], born at Port Jervis, April 13, 1876.

Isaac[8] (139) has eleven children.

330. I. Sarah Ann[9], born at Port Crane, Broome County, New York, February 19, 1853. Died, unmarried, November 29, 1872.
331. II. John Hamilton[9], born at Port Crane, Broome County, New York, February 28, 1855. He is a lumberman and builder, and resides at Killmaster, Alcona County, Michigan; and is at present unmarried.
332. III. Hiram Reuben[9], born at Osborn Hollow, Broome County, New York, September 1, 1856. Married, August 11, 1880, Elizabeth Stone. He is a farmer, and resides at North Fenton, Broome County, New York.
333. IV. Florence Ora[9], born at Osborn Hollow, January 23, 1858. Married, in 1883, Frank Wardell, of Binghamton, New York.
334. V. Jeannette Sylvia[9], born at Osborn Hollow, March 1, 1860. Married, in 1881, James N. Daniels, of Binghamton, New York.
335. VI. Ida Theresa[9], born at Osborn Hollow, November 10, 1861. Married, November 2, 1878, William Storms, of Binghamton.

336. VII. LIZZIE ETTA[9], born at Port Crane, August 21, 1863. She is at present unmarried, and resides at Binghamton.
337. VIII. ALICE E.[9], born at Port Crane, February 15, 1867. She is unmarried, and resides at Binghamton.
338. IX. WILLIS WALTER[9], born at Port Crane, December 2, 1868. He is unmarried, and resides at Killmaster, Alcona County, Michigan.
339. X. MINA MAY[9], born at Port Crane, June 6, 1871. Died March 21, 1876.
340. XI. ISAAC HORACE[9], born at Port Crane, September 17, 1875.

WILLIAM C.[8] (140) has six children.
341. I. HARRIETT ELIZA[9], born in Westchester County, New York, June 19, 1854. Married, February 8, 1880, Charles D. Lockwood. Resides in Van Buren County, Michigan.
342. II. ANSON RUDOLPH[9], born July 19, 1857. Is unmarried, and resides at Minneapolis, Minnesota.
343. III. KATE ELIZABETH[9], born February 26, 1862. Died in infancy.

344. IV. CLARRISSA BELL[9], twin sister of the preceding. Died in infancy.
345. V. WILMINA[9], born June 24, 1864. Died in infancy.
346. VI. OLIVE MARY[9], born May 21, 1866. Died in infancy.

ORVILLE H.[8] (149) has two children.

347. I. CLARENCE[9], born at Newark, Wayne County, New York, in 1849. Died in infancy.
348. II. ORVILLE HURD[9], born at Newark, October 3, 1851. Married, June 3, 1874, Ida C. Leggett, daughter of John T. Leggett, of Newark. From 1873 to 1884, he was engaged in the business of shipping live stock from Western points to New York, and in that year he succeeded his father as Live Stock Agent of the Pennsylvania Railroad. In the summer of 1886 he made a tricycle tour through Scotland, England, Wales and France. He now resides at Pittsburgh, Pennsylvania.

BYRON[8] (151) has two children.

349. I. SAMUEL WATERS[9], born at Newark, Wayne

County, New York, November 2, 1869. He resides at Newark and is unmarried.

350. II. RICHARD HARRISON[9], born at Newark, October 20, 1880.

SAMUEL W.[8] (154) has two children.

351. I. KATE RENNETT[9], born at Chicago, Illinois, June 10, 1863. Married, October 14, 1885, Dr. Francis S. Papin.

352. II. ROBERT HENRY[9], born at Chicago, March 20, 1873.

GEORGE M.[8] (158) had five children.

353. I. GEORGE MILTON[9], born at New York City, January 27, 1860. Married, June 20, 1883, Josephine D. Webster, daughter of Judge J. W. Webster, of Waterbury, Connecticut. He has been connected all his life with the Rubber Manufacturing business, and resides at Waterbury, Connecticut.

354. II. CHARLES GOODYEAR[9], born at New York City, September 9, 1862.

355. III. LOUIS MOTT[9], born at New York City, February 11, 1865.

356. IV. ANNA OGDEN[9], born at Naugatuck, Connecticut, October 14, 1877.

357. V. Robert Wade[9], born at Naugatuck, Connecticut, August 14, 1882.

Reuben G.[8] (159) had three children.

358. I. Nettie Fenton[9], born at New York City, February 4, 1868.
359. II. Atherton[9], born at New York City, November 3, 1869.
360. III. Reuben[9], born at New York City, January 25, 1876.

Henry[8] (164) has one child.

361. I. Adaline Spaulding[9], born at Brooklyn, Connecticut, September 9, 1871.

Samuel[8] (168) had seven children.

362. I. Job D.[9], born in Sandy Township, Stark County, Ohio, September 4, 1838. Married, March 12, 1863, Sarah A. Smith. In 1866, he moved to Indiana, and became a farmer, but afterwards was ordained a minister of the Baptist Church, and is now located at Mentone, Kosciusko County, Indiana.
363. II. Cordelia A.[9], born at Osnaburgh, Stark County, Ohio, October 10, 1840. Died February 24, 1843.

364. III. ANDREW O.⁹, born in Paris Township, Stark County, September 9, 1842. He was a farmer at the outbreak of the Rebellion, when he enlisted in the Union Army, and was killed at Murfreesboro, Tennessee, November 30, 1864. He was never married.

365. IV. CLARA E.⁹, born at Osnaburgh, February 5, 1845. Married, June 1, 1871, Wesley Delap, and resides at Osnaburgh, Stark County, Ohio.

366. V. SAMUEL⁹, born at Osnaburgh, Stark County, March 26, 1847. Died August 12, 1847.

367. VI. ALLEN W.⁹, born at Uniontown, Stark County, February 28, 1849. Married, October 2, 1875, Alice Wilson. He is a painter, and resides in Sandy Township, Stark County.

368. VII. AMOS V.⁹, born at Mapleton, Stark County, October 14, 1851. Married, February 26, 1873, Mary C. Young. He is a mason and builder, also an auctioneer, and resides at Osnaburgh, Stark County, Ohio.

JAMES⁸ (180) has seven children.

369. I. REUBEN⁹, born in Pike Township, Stark County, Ohio, November 16, 1858. He is at present unmarried, and is not engaged

in any business. Resides at Nashville, Barry County, Michigan.

370. II. FRANCIS M.[9], born in Pike Township, August 16, 1860. Married, September 19, 1884, Caroline Carbaugh, of Orange, Iona County, Michigan. He is a farmer, and resides in Castleton Township, Barry County, Michigan.

371. III. ALVIRA[9], born in Pike Township, February 27, 1864. Married, September 26, 1884, Riley Holston, of Piatt County, Illinois. Died December 6, 1886.

372. IV. JOHN A.[9], born in Pike Township, January 20, 1866. Died September 3, 1867.

373. V. ADA A.[9], born in Pike Township, March 18, 1870.

374. VI. LODEMA[9], born at Nashville, Barry County, Michigan, August 16, 1880.

375. VII. LAURA W.[9], born at Nashville, August 26, 1883.

ISAAC CHAUNCEY[8] (185) had one child.

376. I. CHLOE[9], who married Simeon Blocker.

OLIVER H. PERRY[8] (186) has five children.

377. I. ALVAH[9], born at Lake Mills, Jefferson

County, Wisconsin, November 29, 1854. Married, March 3, 1880, Anna A. Nickleson. He had no children and died November 23, 1880.

378. II. JASPER W.[9], born in Waupaca County, Wisconsin, April 30, 1857. Married, November 26, 1881, the widow of his brother Alvah. Is a carpenter and joiner, and resides at Eureka, Winnebago County, Wisconsin.

379. III. EFFIE[9], born at Lake Mills, January 5, 1862. Married, July 27, 1880, Frank H. Fellows.

380. IV. HERBERT[9], born at Lake Mills, Wisconsin, November 7, 1864.

381. V. FREELING C.[9], born at Lake Mills, Wisconsin, January 4, 1867.

ALPHEUS B.[8] (187) has two children.

382. I. EVA M.[9], born at Aztalon, Wisconsin, August 15, 1854. Married, December 19, 1875, Albert E. Jenks.

383. II. ATTILA G.[9], born at Dayton, Wisconsin, February 3, 1859. Married, September 25, 1882, Eudora Burdick. Resides at Hamelin, Browne County, Kansas, and is a farmer and breeder of live stock.

ORVILLE H. ALLERTON.
(149)

THE ALLERTON FAMILY. 133

Amos[8] (195) had six children.

384. I. James W.[9], born at Constantine, St. Joseph County, Michigan, February 15, 1851. Married, October 3, 1875, Margaret Londorf. He is a farmer and resides at Constantine, St. Joseph County, Michigan.

385. II. Mary[9], born at Huntington, Indiana, November 24, 1853.

386. III. William B.[9], born at Huntington, Indiana, September 27, 1855. Married, November 14, 1886, Kate Burger, of Constantine, Michigan. He is a farmer and resides at Constantine.

387. IV. Ida[9], born at Huntington, Indiana, August 14, 1864.

388. V. David[9], born at Huntington, Indiana, May 19, 1858. He is a farmer and resides at Aberdeen, Brown County, Dakota.

389. VI. Ezekiel[9], twin brother of David. He is now employed by the Chicago and Alton Railroad Company.

John[8] (197) had two children.

390. I. Asa[9], born in Huntington County, Indiana, July 30, 1854. Married, October 15, 1879, Sarah Wiles. He is now employed in a

railroad company, and resides at Andrews, Huntington County, Indiana.

391. II. THEODORE[9], born in Huntington County, Indiana, September 23, 1856. Married, January 7, 1882, Ida Breiding, daughter of Henry Breiding, of New Orleans. He travelled through the west and south-west while quite young, and finally settled at New Orleans, and became a manufacturer of boots and shoes. He now resides in that city.

EZEKIEL[8] (202) has two children.

392. I. MARTHA[9], born in Huntington County, Indiana, November 4, 1865. She is at present unmarried, and resides with her parents.

393. II. FRANK[9], born in Huntington County, Indiana, April 8, 1868. He is at present unmarried.

HIRAM[8] (203) has three children.

394. I. DUANE F.[9], born at Van Buren, Hancock County, Ohio, June 20, 1858. Married, July 4, 1879, Calista E. Fisher. He resides at present at Hartford, Michigan.

395. II. Eva[9], born at Smithtown, Mahoning County, Ohio, January 13, 1861. Married, February 24, 1879, Rolla L. Hill, and resides at Hartford, Michigan.

396. III. Lelia[9], born at Hector, Van Buren County, Michigan, August 23, 1865. Married, November 20, 1882, Samuel S. Granger, and resides at Hemingford, Nebraska.

Andrew J.[8] (204) has four children.

397. I. Curtis O.[9], born at Arcadia, Hancock County, Ohio, August 19, 1858. Married, May 23, 1882, Libbie Erwin, of Hartford, Michigan. He is a carpenter and joiner, and resides at Benton Harbor, Berrien County, Michigan.

398. II. Ella E.[9], born at Smithtown, Mahoning County, Ohio, September 16, 1862. Married an engineer named Turner, of Grand Rapids, Michigan.

399. III. Charles B.[9], born at Keelersville, Van Buren County, Michigan, October 5, 1867. He is now a student at Mount Union College, near Alliance, Ohio. Some valuable information for this volume was collected by him.

400. IV. WILLIAM F.⁹, born at Hartford, Michigan, September 11, 1870.

WILLIAM H.⁸ (208) has three children.
401. I. NELLIE O.⁹, born at Alliance, Ohio, May 16, 1870.
402. II. LAURA B.⁹, born at Alliance, August 15, 1872.
403. III. LOUIS⁹, born at Alliance, June 12, 1874.

JOHN⁸ (210) has six children.
404. I. BLANCHE⁹, born at Hartford, Van Buren County, Michigan, March 10, 1878.
405. II. CLARA⁹, born at Hartford, Sept. 13, 1880.
406. III. HOWARD⁹, born at Hartford, July 23, 1882.
407. IV. GEORGE⁹, born at Hartford, June 4, 1884.
408. V. EFFIE⁹, born at Hartford, March 30, 1886.
409. VI. ———⁹, born at Hartford, March 2, 1888.

FRANCIS⁸ (211) has seven children.
410. I. LURA MAUD⁹, born at Lexington, Stark County, Ohio, March 31, 1874.
411. II. OSCAR RAYMOND⁹, born at Alliance, Ohio, April 24, 1876.
412. III. WALTER MELLVILLE⁹, born at Alliance, April 5, 1878.

THE ALLERTON FAMILY.   137

413. IV. EARL WAYNE⁹, born at Alliance, March 6, 1881.
414. V. WARREN ELSWORTH⁹, born at Lexington, Ohio, December 29, 1882.
415. VI. ACEL HOWARD⁹, born at Chase City, Mecklenburg County, Virginia, April 2, 1884.
416. VII. LIONNE MAY⁹, born at Hartford, Van Buren County, Michigan, June 23, 1887.

IRA⁸ (220) has three children.

417. I. HANNAH ESTHER⁹, born at Bellevue, Eaton County, Michigan, May 26, 1868. Died in infancy.
418. II. WARREN W.⁹, born at Bellevue, June 9, 1859. Died in infancy.
419. III. Died in infancy, unnamed.

JOHN⁸ (223) had three children.

420. I. CLAUD L.⁹, born May 18, 1870.
421. II. JENNIE S.⁹, born September 25, 1871.
422. III. HERBERT L.⁹, born January 17, 1878.

OLIVER H.⁸ (224) had three children.

423. I. WILLIAM I.⁹, born at Poland, Ohio, July 29, 1850. Died July 3, 1880.

424. II. WELTHA ANN[9], born at East Fairfield, Columbiana County, Ohio, February 20, 1852. Married Robert Rheard, of Akron, Ohio.

425. III. WINFIELD SCOTT[9], born at East Fairfield, March 8, 1854. Married, April 16, 1884, Kittie Lynch, of Cleveland, Ohio. He is a machinist and resides at Cleveland.

SAMUEL[8] (230) had nine children.

426. I. JOHN W.[9], born at Alliance, Ohio, December 5, 1853. Died October 17, 1854.

427. II. MARY E.[9], born at Mt. Union, Ohio, December 15, 1854. Is unmarried and resides at Philadelphia.

428. III. EMMA A.[9], born at Cleveland, Ohio, November 16, 1856. Married, April 27, 1882, L. G. Logue. Resides at Pittsburgh, Pa.

429. IV. CORA[9], born October 13, 1858. Died in infancy.

430. V. ALICE[9], born at Alliance, July 8, 1860. Died in infancy.

431. VI. HANNAH M.[9], born at Alliance, Ohio, April 20, 1861. Married, June 19, 1883, Charles E. Buttolph. Resides at Mount Union, Stark County, Ohio.

432. VII. RACHEL C.[9], born at Alliance, Ohio, January 3, 1864. Married, October 23, 1884, John W. Way. Resides at Salem, Ohio.
433. VIII. SAMUEL ELLSWORTH[9], born at Massillon, Ohio, October 10, 1866. He is a machinist, resides at Alliance, Ohio, and is at present unmarried.
434. IX. PERCY P.[9], born at Massillon, Ohio, June 24, 1868. Died at Salem, Ohio, March 8, 1877.

ZACHARIAH[8] (231) has seven children.

435. I. WILLIAM[9], born at Alliance, Ohio, January 24, 1853. Died August 5, 1853.
436. II. JOHN[9], born at Alliance, February 15, 1855. Died February 10, 1856.
437. III. EDWARD[9], born at Alliance, January 22, 1858. He is a molder by trade and resides at Alliance. He is at present unmarried.
438. IV. FRANK[9], born at Alliance, June 6, 1860. Died in November, 1872.
439. V. MARY[9], born at Princeton, Indiana, July 12, 1863. Married, December 15, 1879, John Beesler, of Alliance, Ohio.
440. VI. CHARLES[9], born at Cleveland, Ohio, April 8, 1869. Died in November, 1872.

441. VII. JAMES⁹, born at Cleveland, Ohio, May 9, 1871. Died in November, 1872.

WILLIAM⁸ (233) has nine children.

442. I. HENRIETTA⁹, born at Alliance, Ohio, June 1, 1856. Married David Carson, of New Castle, Pennsylvania.
443. II. LUCRETIA⁹, born at Pomeroy, Ohio, September 18, 1857. Married J. T. McKee, of New Lisbon, Ohio.
444. III. JOHN A.⁹, born at Pomeroy, March 4, 1860. He is a machinist, and resides at New Castle, Lawrence County, Pennsylvania.
445. IV. FLORA B.⁹, born at Pomeroy, February 10, 1863. She is unmarried, and resides with her parents.
446. V. BENJAMIN F.⁹, born at Jeffersonville, Ohio, January 10, 1865.
447. VI. WILLIAM⁹, born at Mount Carmel, Illinois. Died in infancy.
448. VII. DORA⁹, born at Princeton, Indiana, August 8, 1874.
449. VIII. CLAUD⁹, born at Princeton, August 8, 1874.
450. IX. ZACHARIAH⁹, born at Princeton, June, 1876.

IDA AND EDITH ALLERTON.
(487 and 488)

ENOCH[8] (234) had one child.

451. I. FLORENCE[9], born at Cincinnati, Ohio. Died in infancy.

ISAAC[8] (240) has five children.

452. I. MARY BELL[9], born at Dell Roy, Carroll County, Ohio, May 21, 1878. Died May 13, 1879.
453. II. LULA V.[9], born at Dell Roy, March 1, 1880. Died May 23, 1882.
454. III. ALLEN[9], born at Dell Roy, March 1, 1882.
455. IV. DORA JANE[9], born at Dell Roy, November 13, 1884.
456. V. CLIDE[9], born at Dell Roy, May 5, 1887.

THE TENTH GENERATION.

RANSOM W.^{9} (249) has three children.

457. I. ESTHER JANE^{10}, born at Gay Head, Greene County, New York, July 10, 1865.
458. II. ELBERT C.^{10}, born at Gay Head, April 7, 1869.
459. III. WILLIAM F.^{10}, born at Gay Head, January 11, 1879.

LEONARD G.^{9} (250) has two children.

460. I. CHARLES GERMAN^{10}, born at Gay Head, Greene County, New York, November 11, 1869.
461. II. JASPER M.^{10}, born at Gay Head, September 17, 1874.

WILLIAM M.^{9} (256) has two children.

462. I. FRANK MEAD^{10}, born at Wenona, Marshall County, Illinois, September 17, 1883.
463. II. RAYMOND G.^{10}, born at Wenona, February 21, 1885.

FRANK C.[9] (265) has four children.

464. I. GRACE[10], born at Thurston, Steuben County, New York, March 17, 1878.
465. II. MAUD[10], born at Thurston, May 4, 1881.
466. III. ANNA[10], born at Thurston, March 29, 1883.
467. IV. OTTA[10], born at Thurston, October 12 1887.

FREDERICK W.[9] (277) has one child.

468. I. ELLEN C.[10], born March 12, 1886. Died September 12, 1886.

FRANK H.[9] (281) has one child.

469. I. FREDERICK P.[10], born at Elmira, New York, March 5, 1875. Died August 11, 1875.

GEORGE W.[9] (286) has six children.

470. I. BESSIE LOUISE[10], born at New York City, March 5, 1867.
471. II. HENRY READ[10], born at New York City, January 20, 1869.
472. III. CHARLOTTE FISH[10], born at New York City, May 8, 1871.
473. IV. ALICE JUDD[10], born at New York City, April 20, 1873. Died December 9, 1879.

474. V. Mary Greenwood[10], born at Brooklyn, New York, June 23, 1881.
475. VI. George Washington[10], born at Brooklyn, July 28, 1883.

David D.[9] (290) has one child.

476. I. Frank M.[10], born at Jersey City, July 1, 1887. Died December 20, 1887.

David[9] (302) has four children.

477. I. Julia Butler[10], born at Yonkers, New York, July 3, 1880. Died August 9, 1881.
478. II. Esther Hurd[10], born at Wethersfield, Connecticut, March 24, 1882.
479. III. David[10], born at Wethersfield, September 6, 1883.
480. IV. Frederick Salisbury[10], born at Wethersfield, December 12, 1884.

Walter S.[9] (303) has one child.

481. I. Adelaide Hersom[10], born at Brooklyn, New York, November 19, 1884.

Rufus M.[9] (304) has one child.

482. I. Rufus King[10], born at Whitneys Point, Browne County, New York, June 6, 1883.

WILLIAM H.[9] (318) has one child.

483. I. ETHEL[10], born at Port Jervis, New York, April 26, 1886.

GEORGE O.[9] (324) has one child.

484. I. JAMES M.[10], born at Port Jervis, New York, May 1, 1881.

HIRAM R.[9] (332) has two children.

485. I. MILLER S.[10], born at North Fenton, Broome County, New York, August 16, 1881.
486. II. HIRAM LEWIS[10], born at North Fenton, February 9, 1884.

ORVILLE H.[9] (348) has two children.

487. I. IDA MAY[10], born at Pittsburgh, Pennsylvania, April 17, 1882.
488. II. EDITH MARIE[10], born at Pittsburgh, January 11, 1887.

GEORGE M.[9] (353) has three children.

489. I. ELSIE WEBSTER[10], born at Naugatuck, Connecticut, April 13, 1884.
490. II. LOIS MABBETT[10], born at Waterbury, Connecticut, March 12, 1886.

491. III. GEORGE MILTON[10], born at Waterbury, May 31, 1888.

JOB D.[9] (362) has one child.
492. I. CLARA[10], born at New Berlin, Stark County, Ohio, March, 1864.

ALLEN W.[9] (367) has three children.
493. I. CHARLES C.[10], born in Sandy Township, Stark County, Ohio, July 24, 1876.
494. II. EDWARD E.[10], born in Sandy Township, November 9, 1878.
495. III. LUCRETIA[10], born in Sandy Township, October 2, 1881.

AMOS V.[9] (368) has seven children.
496. I. AMELIA ALICE[10], born at Osnaburgh, Stark County, Ohio, October 1, 1873.
497. II. WARREN WALTER[10], born at Osnaburgh, February 23, 1875.
498. III. GERTRUDE GROVE[10], born at Osnaburgh, May 9, 1877.
499. IV. LUCINDA LEORA[10], born at Osnaburgh, November 18, 1879.
500. V. SUSAN CORDELIA[10], born at Osnaburgh, February 27, 1881. Died in infancy.

501. VI. BESSIE BEATRICE[10], born at Osnaburgh, May 11, 1883.
502. VII. SAMUEL SIDNEY[10], born at Osnaburgh, October 21, 1886.

FRANCIS M.[9] (370) has one child.
503. I. ETHEL[10], born in Castleton Township, Barry County, Michigan, February 20, 1888.

JASPER W.[9] (378) has three children.
504. I. HATTIE F.[10], born at Rushford, Wisconsin, October 10, 1883.
505. II. WILLIS LEIGH[10], born at Eureka, Winnebago County, Wisconsin, October 31, 1885.
506. III. VOLNEY[10], born at Eureka, September 26, 1887.

ATTILA G.[9] (383) has one child.
507. I. FREDERICK RUSSELL[10], born at Hamlin, Brown County, Kansas, January 18, 1883.

JAMES W.[9] (384) has two children.
508. I. DAISY[10], born at Huntington, Indiana, August 1, 1876.
509. II. MINNIE[10], born in Cass County, Michigan, January 2, 1878.

Asa[9] (390) has four children.

510. I. Emma A.[10], born in Huntington County, Indiana, July 10, 1880.
511. II. Henry[10], born in Huntington County, Indiana, September 6, 1883.
512. III. Fay[10], born in Huntington County, Indiana, June 23, 1886.
513. IV. Fern[10], twin sister of Fay.

Theodore[9] (391) has three children.

514. I. William[10], born at New Orleans, Louisiana, October 19, 1882.
515. II. Henrietta[10], born at New Orleans, March 16, 1885.
516. III. ——[10], born at New Orleans, July 26, 1887.

Duane[9] (394) has one child.

517. I. Wanzer D.[10], born at Keelersville, Michigan, March 18, 1881.

Curtis O.[9] (397) has one child.

518. I. Henry W.[10], born at Keelersville, Michigan, December 17, 1883.

ALLERTONS IN THE UNITED STATES WHO ARE NOT DESCENDANTS OF ISAAC[2].

WILLIAM ALLERTON, born at Birmingham, England, June 8, 1801, who is believed to have been a descendant of Bartholomew[2], the oldest son of Isaac[1], came to Massachusetts in 1815. He married September 23, 1822, Ruth Cutler Thomas, of Provincetown, Massachusetts. He was a ship-master, and died at Gloucester, April 13, 1880. He had twelve children as follows:

I. CAROLINE, born at Provincetown, November 7, 1823. Died March 9, 1838.
II. ORSAMUS THOMAS, born at Provincetown, August 17, 1825. Married, July 17, 1853, Louisa L. Perham, who died in 1857; married again, November 9, 1861, Louisa Wonson. Like his father he was a ship-master, and a man highly esteemed in the community in which he resided. He died at Gloucester, February 14, 1868.
III. EXPERIENCE PARKER, born at Provincetown, October 6, 1828.

IV. ABIGAIL BEALS, born at Provincetown, December 4, 1830.
V. RUTH HINCKLEY, born at Provincetown, August 20, 1833. Died December 17, 1844.
VI. ELIZABETH SCOTT, born at Provincetown, June 25, 1836. Died April 28, 1879.
VII. WILLIAM JAMES, born at Provincetown, July 10, 1838. Died November 12, 1838.
VIII. CAROLINE, twin sister of William J. Died December 1, 1838.
IX. MARY CAROLINE, born at Provincetown, June 20, 1839. Died December 24, 1865.
X. WILLIAM J., born at Provincetown, April, 1842. Died in infancy.
XI. RUTH B., born at Provincetown, February 7, 1845. Died April 10, 1887.
XII. WILLIAM, born at Provincetown, July 14, 1848. Died August 14, 1849.

ORSAMUS T. ALLERTON had two children.
I. WILLIAM, born at Gloucester, Massachusetts, April 14, 1855. He is a manufacturer of picture and mirror frames at Boston, and is at present unmarried.
II. ORSAMUS T., born at Gloucester, December 4, 1865. Died December 8, 1865.

JOHN W. ALLERTON, born at Newark, New Jersey, in 1854, is the son of James A. Allerton, who came to this country about 1840, and died in Newark in 1865. He is at present a resident of Providence, Rhode Island. He married Alfretta E. Bailey, but has no children.

JAMES A. ALLERTON also had two daughters, LETITIA M., born in 1851, and SARAH E., born in 1856, both of whom are now living.

THOMAS ALLERTON, a son of Charles Allerton, of Ashby-de-la-Zouch, Derbyshire, England, came to this country in 1879. He is at present a resident of Pittsburgh, Pennsylvania, and has nine children, as follows:

 I. JOHN CHARLES ALLERTON.
 II. WILLIAM ALLERTON.
 III. THOMAS ALLERTON.
 IV. MARY ALLERTON.
 V. AUSTIN ALLERTON.
 VI. HENRY ALLERTON.
 VII. BENJAMIN NEWBOLD ALLERTON.
 VIII. COLIN ALLERTON.
 IX. ARNOLD ENGLAND ALLERTON.

GEORGE ALLERTON,
SAMSON ALLERTON and
WILLIAM H. ALLERTON,
Are three English potters, who reside at Trenton, New Jersey.

INDEX.

GIVEN NAMES OF ALLERTONS.

	PAGE		PAGE
Abigail	77	Alvira	104
Abigail B.	150	Alvira	131
Abigail M.	106	Amanda	93
Abby	97	Amaryllis	73
Abby L.	119	Amaryllis	93
Acel	137	Ambrose	124
Ada	131	Amelia	146
Adaline	82	Amos	64
Adaline J.	113	Amos	76
Adaline S.	129	Amos	98
Adelaide	144	Amos	99
Adella	124	Amos	102
Admetus	106	Amos V.	130
Allen	141	Amy B.	120
Allen W.	130	Anna	59
Alexander	124	Anna	62
Alice	62	Anna	68
Alice	87	Anna	111
Alice	138	Anna	143
Alice E.	126	Anna O.	128
Alice J.	143	Annie	96
Alice R.	117	Annette	114
Alice R.	119	Andrew J.	104
Almond	105	Andrew O.	130
Almyra	85	Angelina	84
Almyra P.	119	Anson	72
Alpheus B.	101	Anson M.	87
Alvah	131	Anson R.	126

INDEX.

	PAGE		PAGE
Archibald M.	69	Charles H.	88
Archibald M.	88	Charles H.	119
Archibald M.	120	Charles H.	119
Arnold	151	Charlotte A.	122
Asa	102	Charlotte B.	117
Asa	133	Charlotte F.	143
Atherton	129	Chauncey	124
Attila	132	Chloe	100
Augusta	112	Chloe	131
Austin	151	Clara	95
		Clara	136
Bartholomew	22, 48, 149	Clara	146
Benjamin F.	140	Clara E.	10, 130
Benjamin N.	151	Clarissa	89
Betsey	64	Clarissa B.	127
Bessie B.	147	Clarence	127
Bessie L.	143	Claud	140
Blanche	136	Claud L.	137
Byron	94	Clide	141
		Colin	151
Calista	110	Cora	138
Caroline	83	Cordelia	129
Caroline	84	Cornelia	92
Caroline	149	Cornelius	17, 72
Caroline	150	Cornelius	17, 92
Caroline E.	113	Curtis	135
Catherine	107		
Catherine L.	106	Daisy	147
Charles	97	Daniel	99
Charles	139	David	61
Charles	151	David	76
Charles B.	10, 135	David	87
Charles B.	115	David	99
Charles C.	146	David	120
Charles G.	128	David	133
Charles G.	142	David	144

INDEX.

	PAGE		PAGE
David D.	118	Emma E.	86
David S.	103	Emily	85
Delanson	83	Emily	114
Dora	140	Enoch	109
Dora J.	141	Esther	58
Dorcas	100	Esther A.	104
Duane	134	Esther H.	144
Dudley	115	Esther J.	142
		Esther O.	106
Earl	137	Ethel	145
Edith	112	Ethel	147
Edith M.	145	Eva	135
Edward	139	Eva M.	132
Edward E.	146	Experience	149
Effie	132	Ezra	85
Effie	136	Ezekiel	10, 103
Elbert	142	Ezekiel	133
Eleanor	98		
Eleanor	108	Fay	148
Eleanor L.	123	Fern	148
Elipha	95	Flora	140
Eliza A.	83	Florence	111
Eliza J.	120	Florence	141
Eliza M.	118	Florence O.	125
Elizabeth	45, 51	Frank	134
Elizabeth	45, 53	Frank	139
Elizabeth	58	Frank C.	114
Elizabeth	75	Frank H.	117
Elizabeth	99	Frank M.	142
Elizabeth	115	Frank M.	144
Elizabeth S.	150	Frances	89
Ella	135	Frances A.	97
Ellen	143	Frances C.	115
Elsie	145	Francis	85
Emma A.	138	Francis	105
Emma A.	148	Francis M.	131

INDEX.

	PAGE		PAGE
Freeling	132	Hannah M.	138
Freelove	63	Hannah R.	107
Frederick M.	111	Harriet	113
Frederick P.	143	Harriet E.	126
Frederick R.	147	Hattie	147
Frederick S.	122	Henrietta	140
Frederick S.	144	Henrietta	148
Frederick W.	116	Henry	14, 97
Friend	105	Henry	148
		Henry	151
George	75	Henry R.	93
George	115	Henry R.	143
George	136	Henry W.	148
George	152	Herbert	132
George C.	85	Herbert L.	137
George M.	95	Hester	103
George M.	128	Hiram	103
George M.	146	Hiram L.	145
George O.	124	Hiram R.	125
George R.	122	Horace	89
George W.	86	Howard	136
George W.	101	Huron	116
George W.	109		
George W.	118	Ida	116
George W.	123	Ida	133
George W.	144	Ida M.	145
Grace	66	Ida T.	125
Grace	143	Ira	78
Gertrude A.	124	Ira	98
Gertrude G.	146	Ira	106
Goodwin	17, 74	Ira	124
		Isaac	21
Hannah	66	Isaac	44, 49
Hannah	76	Isaac	53
Hannah	98	Isaac	56
Hannah E.	137	Isaac	57

INDEX.

	PAGE		PAGE
Isaac	67	Job	66
Isaac	17, 70	Job	98
Isaac	91	Job D.	17, 129
Isaac	110	Johanna	39, 45
Isaac C.	100	John	55
Isaac H.	126	John	58
Isabella	10, 109	John	64
		John	65
Jacob	77	John	68
Jacob	109	John	74
Jane	97	John	76
Jane G.	10, 108	John	78
James	72	John	81
James	77	John	85
James	78	John	97
James	82	John	98
James	99	John	102
James	103	John	105
James	108	John	107
James	140	John	139
James A.	151	John A.	131
James D.	117	John A.	140
James M.	10, 18, 90	John B.	90
James M.	113	John C.	151
James M.	142	John H.	125
James W.	133	John L.	78
Jasper M.	142	John R.	75
Jasper W.	132	John P.	108
Jeannette M.	87	John T.	84
Jeannette S.	125	John W.	138
Jennie	137	John W.	151
Jerusha	63	Jonathan	60
Jerusha	74	Josephine	118
Jesse	16, 55	Joshua	67
Jesse	66	Judson	114
Jesse	75	Julia	144

158 INDEX.

	PAGE		PAGE
Kate C.	116	Maria	98
Kate E.	126	Mariah	82
Kate R.	128	Margaret	118
		Mary	22, 49
		Mary	58
Lamar	114	Mary	76, 78
Laura B.	136	Mary	92
Laura W.	131	Mary	101
Lavinia	76	Mary	103
Leander	83	Mary	111
Lelia	135	Mary	116
Lemira	10, 107	Mary	133
Leonard	112	Mary	139
Letitia	151	Mary	151
Lewis	119	Mary A.	75
Lionne	137	Mary A.	86
Lizzie C.	117	Mary A.	97
Lizzie E.	126	Mary A.	98
Lodema	113	Mary B.	141
Lodema	131	Mary C.	113
Lois J.	94	Mary C.	150
Lois M.	145	Mary E.	95
Louis	136	Mary E.	109
Louis M.	128	Mary E.	116
Lucinda	146	Mary E.	123
Lucretia	140	Mary E.	138
Lucretia	146	Mary G.	118
Lucy	69	Mary G.	144
Lucy	73	Mary J.	84
Lucy	112	Mary J.	89
Lucy A.	81	Mary K.	104
Lucy A.	82	Mary L.	106
Lucy B.	86	Mary L.	122
Lula	141	Mary M.	123
Lura	136	Mary S.	122
Luthera	114	Matilda	123

INDEX.

	PAGE		PAGE
Martha	134	Ransom	15, 81
Maud	143	Ransom W.	112
Maurice	124	Raymond	142
Mead	7, 10, 15, 80	Rebecca	94
Miller	145	Remember	22, 48
Milton	74	Reuben	17, 62
Mina	126	Reuben	17, 69
Minnie	119	Reuben	92
Minnie	147	Reuben	129
Mira	74	Reuben	130
		Reuben G.	96
Nancy	72	Reuben G.	113
Nettie	129	Rhoda	77
Nellie	136	Richard	128
Norman	125	Robert H.	128
		Robert W.	129
Olive	127	Roger	63
Oliver H.	107	Rose	64
Oliver H. P.	100	Rosanna	99
Orsamus T.	149	Rufus K.	121
Orsamus T.	150	Rufus K.	144
Orville H.	10, 93	Russell	64
Orville H.	127	Russell	18, 74
Oscar	136	Ruth B.	150
Otta	143	Ruth H.	150
Pamela	77	Sally	72
Percy	139	Sally	84
Polly	70	Samson	152
Polly	73	Samuel	65
Polly	77	Samuel	79
Rachel	77	Samuel	98
Rachel	102	Samuel	108
Rachel B.	122	Samuel	130
Rachel C.	139	Samuel E.	139
Rachel E.	110	Samuel S.	147

INDEX.

	PAGE		PAGE
Samuel W.	19, 73	Volney	147
Samuel W.	94		
Samuel W.	127	Walter M.	113
Sarah	22, 36, 49	Walter M.	136
Sarah	22, 49	Walter S.	18, 121
Sarah	59	Warren E.	137
Sarah	63	Warren W.	137
Sarah	63	Warren W.	146
Sarah	68	Wanzer	148
Sarah	81	Weltha	138
Sarah	102	William	75
Sarah	108	William	109
Sarah	115	William	139
Sarah A.	89	William	140
Sarah A.	125	William	148
Sarah C.	123	William	149
Sarah E.	151	William	150
Sarah H.	92	William	150
Sarah J.	101	William	151
Serena	86	William B.	122
Sophia	115	William B.	133
Sophronia	102	William C.	82
Stephen	65	William C.	87
Stephen W.	105	William C.	91
Susan	124	William C.	119
Susan C.	146	William F.	136
Sybil	101	William F.	142
Sylvia	123	William H.	104
		William H.	123
Teressa	106	William H.	152
Theodore	134	William I.	137
Theron	111	William J.	150
Thomas	79	William J.	150
Thomas	151	William M.	113
Thomas	151	Willis L.	147
Townsend	83	Willis R.	117

	PAGE		PAGE
Willis W.	126	Zachariah	59
Wilmina	127	Zachariah	108
Winfield	138	Zachariah	140

SURNAMES OTHER THAN ALLERTON.

	PAGE		PAGE
Adams, Amelia S.	90	Belden, Taber	74
Alexander, William	106	Berry, John B.	122
Albro, ——	63	Betts, Cyrastus	82
Allen, Edward P.	120	Betts, Letitia	112
Amory, Rufus K.	87	Bingham, Hamilton	119
Andress, Polly	68	Billington, John	27
Andrews, James M.	114	Blackmar, Lavinia	80
Atherton, Lois	62	Blocker, Simeon	131
Austin, Ann M.	87	Brassen, Henry	44
Avery, Rev. ——	37	Bradford, William 22, 25, 28, 31, 32, 36	
Babcock, Isaac	104	Bramm, Gustavus	123
Babcock, Martha	104	Breiding, Henry	134
Baker, George	124	Breiding, Ida	134
Bailer, Lois	104	Brewster, Fear	29
Bailer, Peter	104	Brewster, Patience	29
Bailey, Alfretta E.	151	Brewster, William. 25, 27, 29, 44	
Barnaby, Joshua	104	Brown, Peter	27
Barlow, Thomas	73	Bryan, George	83
Barrett, Molly	64	Bryan, Jane	83
Bassett, Polly	67	Bryan, Joshua	84
Baughman, Mary	79	Bullock, Benjamin	69
Baum, Rebecca	102	Burdick, Eudora	132
Beaton, George	114	Burger, Kate	133
Beesler, John	139	Burlingame, Rose	58
Belden, Eliza	74	Burmiston, William C.	117

INDEX.

	PAGE
Burns, Frank	124
Buttolph, Charles E	138
Campbell, Amanda	107
Campbell, Samuel	64
Carr, Aaron H	116
Carbaugh, Caroline	131
Carson, David	140
Carver, John	25, 26, 28
Chamberlain, Rebecca	70
Chapin, Ahira	83
Chapin, Ann	83
Chapman, Ann H	111
Collson, Emma	114
Colson, Luvina R	81
Cooke, Francis	27
Cook, James	81
Cooper, John	40
Cooper, Rose	58
Corfield, William	51
Cradock, ——	37
Crage, Rachel	65
Cushman, Thomas	28, 49
Daniels, James N	125
Darke, Isaac D	118
Dawson, Harriet A	72
Dean, Eliza A	93
Delap, Clara E	10, 130
Delap, Wesley	130
Denius, Levi	102
Dobbin, Margaret R	86
Dudley, Mary J	83
Dunham, Isaac	72
Durland, Clark	89

	PAGE
Edwards, John A	119
Eggleston, Hamilton	89
Eggleston, Nicholas	89
Erwin, Libbie	135
Evans, ——	41
Evans, Gervase	86
Eyres, Elizabeth	45, 53
Eyres, Simon	39, 51, 53
Fellows, Frank H	132
Fisher, Calista E	134
Fitch, ——	62
Fuller, Seneca	101
Fulmer, Samuel	102, 103
Gage, Levi	85
German, Reuben	68
Gibson, Margaret	103
Giddings, Elvira A	100
Glines, Fanny	100
Godbertson, Godbert	36, 49
Goble, Mary E	90
Goffe, ——	45
Goodman, John	27
Gorham, Augusta	88
Granger, Samuel S	135
Green, Jane A	82
Guthrie, Eliza	116
Guthrie, Jennie	116
Hall, Thomas	43
Hand, Marcia L	85
Hanson, Fannie E	105
Harding, Sarah	124
Harriman, John	43
Harman, Augustus	43

INDEX. 163

	PAGE		PAGE
Hartshorn, E. N.	104	Irish, Lavinia	121
Hartzell, Sarah	108	Irish, Samuel K.	121
Hatherly, Timothy	33		
Haynes, John	38	James, George	63
Headley, Joseph	98	Jenks, Albert E.	132
Hemingway, Hiram G.	84	Joseph, John	109
Hersom, Adelaide L.	121	Judd, Elizabeth R.	118
Hersom, Andrew J.	121	Judd, William	118
Hess, Peter M.	85		
Heusted, Clarissa	73	Kellogg, Eleanor	78
Hewlett, Edmund P.	115	Kieft, Gov.	38
Hill, Harvey	106	Kinnel, Emanuel	103
Hill, Rolla L.	135	Knapp, Mary	109
Hoagg, Mary A.	106	Knight, Jennie E.	90
Hoagg, Samuel G.	106	Koon, John	83
Hoffman, Alice T.	117	Kynett, James	109
Hogg, Thomas	106	Kynett, Mrs. James	10, 109
Hoge, Hannah	113		
Holcomb, Ebenezer L.	83	Lafarge, Elizabeth	92
Holden, Henry F.	106	Laughlin, Sophronia	76
Holston, Riley	131	Leatherdale, Luke	101
Hook, John	22	Lee, Hancock	51, 54
Hooper, William B.	120	Lee, Richard	51, 54
House, Addison	100	Leggett, Ida C	127
Hoyt, Amanda	101	Leggett, John T.	127
Hufman, Martha	78	Leggett, Mary A.	95
Hungerford, Hannah	85	Lockwood, Charles D.	126
Hungerford, Marian	122	Lockwood, Tamar H.	87
Huntington, Eliza A.	82	Logue, L. G.	138
Hurd, Hannah	73	Londorf, Margaret	133
Hurd, Hebron	87	Ludwick, Jacob	90
Hurd, Rachel W.	87	Lupper, John	77
Hustace, William A.	120	Lutz, Catharine	65
Hutson, H. D.	10	Lynch, Kittie	138
Husong, Mary	76		
Hyer, Perry	101	Mabbett, Lois	95

INDEX.

	PAGE		PAGE
Mackey, Hetta	78	Otter, Ann E.	89
Martin, ——	72	Owen, Calvin	72
Massasoit	28		
Mathews, Mary E.	118	Paine, Robert	41
Mathews, William S.	118	Palmer, Ellen P.	101
Maverick, Moses	36, 37, 49	Papin, Francis S.	128
McCoy, Sarah	107	Parks, Bathsheba	70
McDaniel, Eliza	91	Parker, Adam	115
McDaniel, Hiram	91	Partello, Eva	109
McDonnel, William	98	Patterson, ——	76
McKee, Elizabeth	109	Peigh, Nancy	102
McKee, J. T.	140	Pemble, John	98
McLaughlin, Susan	110	Perham, Louisa L.	149
Mead, Bathsheba	60	Perry, ——	40
Mead, Joshua	60	Peterson, John	44
Mead, Samuel B.	119	Petrie, George H.	95
Meaker, William	41	Phillips, Elsie	63
Merritt, William	118	Pierce, ——	35
Miller, Maria	69	Plank, Addison J.	117
Mitchner, Jane G.	108	Pool, Elizabeth	79
Montgomery, Janet	61	Porter, Abby M.	97
Montgomery, Gen'l Rich'd	61	Preston, Edward	43
Morton, William	34	Priest, Degory	22, 49
		Purinton, Daniel W.	97
Nash, ——	76		
Nash, Thomas	40	Randall, Addison	107
Neff, Maria	97	Randall, Stephen	108
Nichols, Barnabas A.	84	Ransom, David	62
Nickleson, Anna A.	132	Rapelyea, Caroline	84
Niewander, Mary A.	99	Reeves, ——	77
Nobles, Isaac	114	Rheard, Robert	138
Norris, Mary	22, 26	Robertson, Harriet	100
Norton, John	86	Robson, Charlotte A.	88
		Rogers, Minnie A.	111
Oby, Henrietta	105	Rundell, Lewis	82
Oby, Joseph	105	Runnels, David	62

INDEX.

	PAGE		PAGE
Salisbury, Matilda C.	120	Sweet, Calvin	84
Salisbury, Thomas	120	Swift, Lemuel J.	82
Salmon, John	51	Swope, Amelia	98
Sargent, Sarah T.	108		
Scarlet, Captain	43	Taber, William	93, 94
Scott, Jane	72	Teel, ——	77
Scranton, Amelia	104	Teeters, Richard W.	110
Selden, Dwight	99	Tilden, Charles	100
Sheares, Timothy	99	Tilden, Jasper	10
Sherley, James	32	Thomas, Ruth C.	149
Sherman, Cornelia	111	Thompson, Agnes C.	94
Sherman, Helen	94	Thompson, Pamilla W.	94
Sherman, Shadrac	93	Townsend, Charlotte	68
Sherman, Walter	92, 93	Truex, George E.	123
Short, Seneca	111	Turner, ——	135
Silvers, Mary	77		
Smith, Moses	123	Vanostan, Elizabeth	99
Smith, Sarah A.	129	Vredenbergh, Henrietta L.	96
Spaulding, ——	62	Vredenbergh, Robert M.	96
Spaulding, Adaline	75		
Spaulding, Lucy	57	Wardell, Frank	125
St. John, George B.	106	Warren, Moses	100
Standish, Miles	28	Way, John W.	139
Staples, Ernest	122	Weaver, John	102
Starr, Allerton	53	Webster, J. W.	128
Starr, Benjamin	53	Webster, Josephine D.	128
Stebbins, Ellery	119	Welch, Esther	82
Stebbins, Fitzalan	92	West, ——	63
Stevens, Mary	112	Whalley, ——	45
Stiles, Chloe	65	Wilcox, Philander	70
Stiles, ——	45	Wiles, Sarah	133
Stidd, Antoinette	123	Wilken, Joseph	124
Stone, Elizabeth	125	Wilson, Alice	130
Stone, Howell P.	124	Willett, Captain	43
Storms, William	125	Williams, Charles	123
Sweet, ——	55	Williams, Roger	34

	PAGE		PAGE
Winchell, Martin	71	Woolsey, George.........	44
Winchell, Sylvia.........	71		
Winslow, Edward ...25, 27, 31		Young, John D.	118
Winthrop, John 35, 38		Young, Mary C.	130
Wonson, Louisa	149		

www.ingramcontent.com/pod-product-compliance
Lightning Source LLC
Chambersburg PA
CBHW032145160426
43197CB00008B/776